PROPHET SHARING 2021

PROPHET SHARING 2021

Daneen Bottler
Curt Crook
Ann Finley
Bobby Haaby
Dr. Dan Hammer
Herb Marks
Abbey McCracken
Jeff McCracken
Kathi Pelton
Dr. George Watkins

Inscribe Press
Creativity Unleashed

Fredericksburg, VA

PROPHET SHARING 2021

Copyright © 2020 Rainier Assembly of God.

All rights reserved. No part of this book may be used or reproduced in any manner whatsoever without written permission, except in the case of brief quotations in critical articles and reviews. For more information, contact the publisher at: admin@inscribepress.com.

Published by Inscribe Press, Fredericksburg, VA.
Cover design by Pelton Media Group, Fredericksburg, VA.

Bible versions quoted are as follows.
New King James Version®. Copyright © 1982 by Thomas Nelson.
Used by permission. All rights reserved.
The Holy Bible, New International Version®, NIV®. Copyright © 1973, 1978, 1984, 2011 by Biblica, Inc.™ Used by permission of Zondervan. All rights reserved worldwide. www.zondervan.com The "NIV" and "New International Version" are trademarks registered in the United States Patent and Trademark Office by Biblica, Inc.™
The NEW AMERICAN STANDARD BIBLE®, Copyright © 1960,1962,1963,1 968,1971,1972,1973,1975,1977,1995 by The Lockman Foundation.
Used by permission.
The Passion Translation®. Copyright © 2017, 2018 by Passion & Fire Ministries, Inc. Used by permission. All rights reserved. (ThePassionTranslation.com)
THE MESSAGE, copyright © 1993, 2002, 2018 by Eugene H. Peterson. Used by permission of NavPress. All rights reserved. Represented by Tyndale House Publishers, a Division of Tyndale House Ministries.

ISBN (print): 978-1-951611-17-0
(ebook): 978-1-951611-18-7

Library of Congress Control Number: 2020925513

TABLE OF CONTENTS

Introduction by Jeff McCracken	7
1. Ann Finley—Put On, Take Off, and Stand Firm	13
2. Curt Crook—The Invitation	27
3. Jeff McCracken—A New Beginning	33
4. Dr. George Watkins—Pouring Water on the Sacrifice	49
5. Herb Marks—Tell Them "There is a Future!"	63
6. Dr. Dan Hammer—Five Keys for 2021	69
7. Abbey McCracken—A Vision of the Seven Mountains	81
8. Bobby Haaby—A New Government	87
9. Kathi Pelton—A Wrestle, or a Dance?	123
10. Daneen Bottler—Crossing the Threshold	137
Author Biographies	149

INTRODUCTION
Jeff McCracken

I absolutely love to laugh! So, a couple of years ago, when the Lord whispered the phrase "Prophet Sharing," it made me giggle. Even today, I can't say it without a smile. I just love God's sense of humor.

When I heard the phrase, I didn't know what to do with it other than laugh. I eventually contacted some prophetic friends that I know in the Portland, Oregon area and asked them to meet me for lunch to discuss the phrase and begin an open dialogue. This dialogue has continued in several different manifestations.

In early 2020, I felt a prompting from the Lord to gather some of my friends whom I trust and know can hear from God. I asked them to join me in writing what we sensed was coming that year, and the result was a publication titled *Prophet Sharing 2020*. This took place before Covid-19 and the quarantine, before toilet paper shortages, riots, looting, arson, forest fires, Black Lives Matter, Antifa, eliminate the police, CHOP/CHAZ, governors dictating that we stay in our homes while they flew to Hawaii, etc. When each of us wrote our chapters, we wrote them with what we could see in the spirit realm, which is usually a combination of literal and figurative visions, dreams, sentences, phrases, and more. For instance, I wrote that the church was going to be—and needed to be—re-invented. WOW! I had no idea what that was really going to look like.

Here we are a year later. The church was reinvented the first time online as people watched from their living rooms, probably still in their pajamas and eating their bowl sof cereal. It seemed as though the life and passion was yanked out of the church. Then when we did return in person, according to not only Pew Research but also every pastor that I know, thirty-percent of the people have not gone back to attending services.

I saw this in a vision in spring, 2020 as the Lord showed me a series of concentric circles that looked like a target. It was flat and people were standing on it. The center represented leadership and the circles represented the people's levels of leadership and commitment in the church, all the way out the fringe people that only show up on holidays. I began to see puzzle pieces suddenly dropping out of the circles and the people on top of them disappear. This was happening randomly throughout the circles, including leaders in the middle zones. Sure enough, many churches, including ours, began to experience people from every circle, including key leaders, suddenly dropping out and not coming back. The church was being changed from the inside out.

Now as I write this, it is late November and some states have outlawed in-person church services or minimized the size again. Some have outlawed singing in church. They have designated how and where we can sit and insisted that we have to wear masks. Potlucks, banquets, holiday celebrations, fellowships and home gatherings have all been cancelled. And now, just days before Thanksgiving, officials have outlawed gathering in our homes with family members. They are threatening to send law enforcement to make sure that we cooperate.

I share all of this to say that it was a crazy year to start a book series about what God is saying to us. As the different authors have written for 2021, we wrote from the position of still being in awe of what 2020 actually ended up looking like.

Some would say that we should have seen all this coming. Can I just tell you: it doesn't work that way. The Bible says, "For now we see through a glass, darkly; but then face to face: now I know in part; but then shall I know even as also I am known." (1 Corinthians 13:12) This means that we don't get to see everything clearly, but we are being led by Holy Spirit until we can look face to face with Jesus.

The Bible also says, "Surely the Lord GOD does nothing, Unless He reveals His secret to His servants the prophets." (Amos 3:7) God is still on the move and doing things on the earth. He alerts us through His prophets, but it is not always clear what His work will look like.

The authors of this book have spent time in prayer and have diligently written what they sense God is saying to them. We (the authors) submit ourselves to God and to you. We humbly share what we believe God is saying.

Now you, the reader, have a responsibility. As you read through this book, you are presented with ideas, concepts, and visions. Once these things have been revealed to you, you can reject them, or you can ponder them, pray into them, and stand firm with those you believe are true. You will have to make a decision.

If you don't know Jesus Christ as your Lord and Savior and you are reading this, there is a decision before you right now, before you dive into the rest of the book. God loves you so much that not only did He direct you to this book, but He sent His Son, Jesus Christ, to die on a cross for you. The Bible states that we have all sinned and come short of the glory of God (Romans 3:23). This means that you and I were designed and created to live in God's glory, but because we have sinned (done things that were not right) we have come short of that opportunity. However, because of the sacrifice of Jesus's sinless life on the cross, we can be set free of sin and can live in God's glory by accepting Jesus as our Savior and inviting Him to live in our hearts. We can dedicate the rest of our lives to living for Him.

Just say this prayer, "Jesus, I repent of my sins and I invite you to live in my heart as my Savior. I want you to be Lord and ruler in my life. Thank you for dying for me, so I can live for you."

If you said this and meant it, the Bible says that there is a party in your name going on in Heaven. It also means that you will have eternal life with Jesus. I would encourage you to find a strong Bible-believing, Jesus-loving, Pentecostal or Charismatic church in your area. Here are a few websites that can you help you find one, but please realize that "results may vary."

www.ag.org/Resources/Directories/Find-a-Church

www.foursquare.org/locator/

www.mfileader.org/find-a-church

And now, I present to you *Prophet Sharing 2021*. May God use this to spur you into your destiny!

Working and worshipping while it is still day,
Pastor Jeff McCracken

Ann Finley

Ann grew up with a Catholic background in Lake Oswego, Oregon. As a young adult, she witnessed the power of the prophetic gift in action and knew that the Lord wanted her to run after and "jealously desire" this gift. She met her future husband Don in Bible college, and after graduation they moved to Salem, Oregon to assist in a newly planted church. They became the senior leaders in 1995.

Ann's prophetic voice and burden to see freedom and transformation is communicated in her music, teaching, preaching, and praying. Her desire is for each of us to learn to hear our Lord's voice and be able to communicate it, not just as a "ministry skill" in church, but as a "life skill" wherever we go! This knowledge of who we are and to whom we belong will help us change our environment as we assist in bringing heaven to earth through His supernatural power working in us.

1
PUT ON, TAKE OFF, AND STAND FIRM
Ann Finley

> 2 Chronicles 20:20; "Believe in the Lord your God, and you shall be established; believe His prophets, and you shall prosper."

Many people are profoundly grateful that the year 2020 is over! It was definitely a difficult, trying, and emotional season; one of confusion and turmoil, and what many have deemed a "reset." It seems that everything that could be shaken, has been shaken (Heb. 12:26). After this tumultuous time, if ever there was ever a year that I would want to hear what the prophets are saying…it's NOW! All over the globe, there are many powerful prophetic voices speaking what they sense the Lord is saying for 2021. I preface my chapter by mentioning how honored I am to be part of this book.

> 1 Corinthians 13:9: For we know in part and we prophesy in part.

Even as I write this, the national election for the President of the United States of America is still under investigation and is NOT

OVER. The prophet, Bobby Connor saw in advance that 2020 would include a major "Shake Up for a Wake Up!" I'm a passionate patriot, meaning that I love our country, and am so thankful for the United States of America. I don't worship our country but I love and worship the God upon whom our nation was founded. Honestly, I'm concerned that if we don't stay "one nation under God," we'll become one nation "gone under!"

As a firm believer in the importance of "speaking those things that are not yet, as though they were" (Ro. 4:17); I'm declaring that even through this "shake up," the Covid-19 Pandemic, the ravenous fires, the looting, the riots, the loss of employment, the loss of education, the loss of lives, the compromised relationships as well as the recently described "electionemic," that God is on the throne and what the enemy has meant for evil, the Lord will use for good! (Romans 8:28). It's time for us to "wake up!" So, what's our next step?

Take Off Your Sandals

The book of Joshua teaches that the fulfillment of God's promises of blessing to Israel depended on their faith and obedience. Their journey into Canaan and beyond, through their struggles of conquest, division, and settlement of the promised land, were each dependent upon their actions. The great blessings of victory, inheritance, provision, peace, and rest all came if the people trusted and obeyed God.

> Now when Joshua was near Jericho, he looked up and saw a man standing in front of him and asked, "Are you for us or for our enemies?" "Neither," he replied, "but as commander of the army of the Lord I have now come." Then Joshua fell facedown to the ground in reverence, and asked him, "What message does my Lord have for his servant?" The commander of the Lord's army replied, "Take off your sandals, for the

place where you are standing is holy." And Joshua did so. (Joshua 5:13)

This "man" that appeared to Joshua in this passage, was an Angel of Superior Rank, the Commander of the Lord's army. Some say that he was an appearance of God in human form. Joshua and the Israelites were on assignment from the Lord to take the land. When meeting a strange warrior, he asked the obvious question: Are you for us or against us? This angel's answer is unexpected. He says "neither!" This unusual declaration was a push-back on Joshua. He must have been confused because he was there doing God's work, but he had to humble himself to align with God. We are in similar circumstances: we are on assignment from God, doing the Lord's work of extending His Kingdom; but God is asking us to ponder the same question today: "Am I aligned with God in this situation?"

Joshua was Israel's leader, but he was subordinate to God, the Absolute Leader. In this moment he was confronted with holiness and authority. In awe and respect, Joshua took off his sandals as he was commanded. In the presence of the Holy, we must humble ourselves and lay down our plans and our ideas. Respect for God is just as important today as it was in Joshua's day, even though removing shoes is no longer our regular way of showing it.

Today, we can demonstrate our honor for God through our attitudes and actions. In our continual attempts to recognize God's power, authority, and deep love, our lives must model and accurately "re-present" Him in everything that we say and do.

Joshua's question to the angel, "Are you for us or for our enemies?" was not the right question. More accurately, he should have asked, and we should be asking, "whose side are *we* on?"

In attempts to paraphrase this Scripture passage: "Take off your sandals, for the place where you are standing is holy," I am encouraging us to "take off" our personal opinions and our biases that may be causing unnecessary "distance" with others. I'm referring to the differences that cause us to wrongfully judge and mistreat those with whom we disagree. I am not suggesting that we remove our moral standards or biblical convictions. I'm referring to those areas of thought that come across as pride or even "self-righteousness." In some cases, we must "agree to disagree."

> Our lives must model and accurately "re-present" the Lord in everything that we say and do.

There are spiritual meanings of shoes and sandals in Scripture. Shoes in the Bible can symbolize our direction and life's path. Also, they often symbolize our faith and readiness to be of service to God. Could our opinions be indirectly misleading us or misguiding our paths? With easy access to the internet and people's insatiable desire for immediate information, there are a plethora of "opinions" and paths vying for our attention!

Garris Elkins states so honestly: "When we allow our personal opinions to become doctrine, we will always harm and divide the unity of the Church. At no point in my lifetime have I seen the importance of making that distinction as it has become in this moment of history." ("Prophetic Horizons," *garriselkins.com*)

> Psalm 119:105: "Your word is a lamp unto my feet and a light unto my path."

This Scripture reminds us of the importance of our feet being directed by the Lord's leading. I sense that as we currently experience immense tension in our nation, we are standing on holy ground and we are to remove our own agendas. I'm asking this question: Are we willing to "take off our shoes" and submit our opinions and paths to the Lord? As we agree to "take off" our self-righteous, prideful ways and submit them to God, we must remember that "for though we walk in the flesh, we do not war according to the flesh..." (2 Cor. 10:3). We then need to decide to put on the essential garments that will help move us forward.

Because I'm in charge of the prophetic ministry at LIFE Church in Salem, Oregon, this year I felt it necessary to ask several respected and trusted prophetic voices to pray for a word for our church and our leadership team for 2021. One of these trusted voices is Michael Herron. Mike was our previous pastor, under our former name, Willamette Valley Christian Fellowship. In 1995, Mike asked my husband Don and me to become the senior leaders as he followed the Lord's direction and was released as a prophet to the nations. We agreed and soon changed the name of the church to LIFE Church. Many things have transpired over the years; however Mike is now a member of what we call our "Apostolic Counsel." He regularly lends an important prophetic and fathering voice to our house. When I read Mike Herron's word, my heart burned within me and I knew that it was for the broader body of Christ in this season. The following is part of his prophetic word:

"I sense that God wants to clothe the congregation with the 'Colossians Cloak...'

> Since God chose you to be the holy people he loves, you must clothe yourselves with tender hearted mercy, kindness, humility, gentleness, and patience. Make allowance for each other's faults, and forgive anyone who offends you. Remember, the Lord forgave you, so you must forgive others. Above all, clothe yourselves with love which binds us all together in perfect harmony. And let the peace that comes from Christ rule in your hearts. For as members of one body you are called to live in peace. And always be thankful.
> (Col. 3:12-15, NLT)

"With so much acrimony and hatred building in our society the church needs to focus on these seemingly fragile but ultimately powerful qualities that can only be generated by the Holy Spirit.

Mercy is the fountainhead for all the other attributes. I think your focus on speaking life giving words and not succumbing to condemning those who are different is the pathway forward. It draws people to Jesus and transformation."

Put on the 'Colossians Cloak'
Part of the challenge with prophetic words is our unwillingness to "fight the good fight" and apply the words practically to our lives. Prophetic words are often conditional and require steps of obedience and faith to see them fulfilled.

I'm a huge promoter of "prophetic acts." In other words, I like to take physical, natural steps to demonstrate a spiritual principal. Over a month ago, I was at the beach and ran across a teal rain coat at the outlet mall. Living in Oregon, we can never have too many rain coats! I was drawn to this coat and slipped it on. At first I thought, "you really don't need this, Ann." I left the store, but shortly thereafter, I had the Holy Spirit "nudge" to buy it after all. I did, and within the week, Don asked me to speak to the church on an upcoming Sunday. I knew that this new raincoat was to be used as an illustration. I researched the spiritual meaning of my new coat's color and found that it means:

*Teal combine*s the calming properties of blue with the renewal qualities of green. It is a revitalizing and rejuvenating color that also represents open communication and clarity of thought.

When I read this I thought, "WOW!" Yes, with all the unrest and chaos whirling around us these days, we need the calming and renewal properties of this teal color! Shortly thereafter, I put on the coat as a prophetic act for an illustration while speaking.

No matter how strongly, passionately, or right we feel inside, we must be willing to take off our sandals and put on the "Colossians Cloak"! The truths of each of the qualities contained in Colossians 3:12-15 could be chapters on their own. What we find here is that each one of the qualities mentioned in this passage express themselves in personal relationships. There is no mention of virtues like efficiency or cleverness, not even of diligence or industry—not that these are unimportant—but the great basic Christian virtues are those which govern human relationships.

The following gives a brief description of these seemingly "fragile" but ultimately powerful qualities with which we're to be clothed:

1. Tender Hearted Mercy. If something is tender, it is sensitive to the touch. Here the apostle Paul would have the Colossians feel the slightest touch of another's misery. It is described as compassion; a deep place in our bowels of emotion, longing, and manifestations of pity. How many of you are "feelers"? The recent tragic fires, the loss, the violence and destruction have probably pushed your buttons big time! I know that they have mine; I immediately wanted to DO something to help!

    > No matter how strongly, passionately, or right we feel inside, we must be willing to take off our sandals and put on the "Colossians Cloak"

2. Kindness. Moral goodness and integrity. The ancient writers defined this virtue as existing in the "Man whose neighbor's good is as dear to him as his own." I've had to ask myself, "Ann, what is the 'dearest good' to you? Are you willing to give it up for someone else?"
3. Humility. Modesty; not thinking too highly of ourselves. I love how Kris Vallotton recently wrote in his blog that "Humility is the Way Forward." (https://www.krisvallotton.com/humility-is-the-way-forward). We can say that humility is the "parent" of both gentleness (meekness/quiet strength and patience (longsuffering.)
4. Gentleness/Meekness. Shows how humility will affect my

actions towards others. I will not dominate, manipulate, or coerce for my own ends, even if I have the power and the ability to do so.

5. Patience/Long Suffering. Shows how humility will affect my reaction towards others. I will not become impatient, short-tempered, or filled with resentment towards the weaknesses and sins of others.

6. Make allowance for others' faults. This quality is "'even-tempered" and is content with second place. Being married, I know that my husband Don has the opportunity to "make allowance" for my faults daily!

7. Forgiving one another. We are told to live forgiving one another, after the pattern of Jesus's forgiveness towards us. Then Peter came to Him and said, "Lord how often shall my brother sin against me, and I forgive him? Up to seven times?" Jesus said to him, "I do not say to you, up to seven times, but up to seventy times seven." (Matthew 18:21-22). In other words, don't bother doing the math! Forgive however many times are necessary!

8. Clothe yourself with love. God is love; it is unconditional (Greek: *agape*).

Do you remember the old song, "They will know we are Christians by our love?" Are people recognizing that we are Christians? The Scripture that most closely says this is:

> John 13:35; "For when you demonstrate the same love I have for you by loving one another, everyone will know that you're my true followers"

What is happening in your life in the area of person relationships? We can each attest to the fact that this last year with the Covid pandemic has thrown a challenging "wrench" into our connections. When the Pharisees asked

Jesus a question about the greatest commandment, He was clear to remind them of what was most important.

> "Teacher, which is the greatest commandment in the law? Jesus said to him, 'You shall love the Lord your God with all your heart, with all your soul, and with all your mind.' This is the first and great commandment. And the second is like it; 'You shall love your neighbor as yourself.'" (Matthew 22:36-39)

We know that the enemy has come only to steal, kill, and destroy (See John 10:10). Families have suffered division physically and emotionally, and many arguments and disagreements have ensued. We must continually endeavor to remember that

> Love NEVER fails (1 Corinthians 13:8).

I often think about what the Lord asked Bob Jones when he went to Heaven: "Did you learn to love?" This question frequently comes to my mind. If you're in a relational situation that has been jeopardized by this pandemic, or any other reason, and if those who were once close to you now seem very "far away," I encourage you to "keep your love on" and believe for restoration!

9. Let His peace rule in our hearts. This is His tranquil wholeness. It is the Person of Jesus Himself...surrender and ask Him to "take the wheel!"
10. Always be thankful.

> In everything give thanks; for this is the will of God in Christ Jesus for you. (1 Thessalonians 5:18)

"In everything give thanks...Thanksgiving accomplishes the divine justice of the Kingdom, where the enemy is destroyed by the very thing he intended to use for our destruction." (Bill Johnson, *Strengthen Yourself in the Lord*.)

In everything give thanks...yikes, even now? It is the Lord's will for us to thank Him even in the midst of the most difficult times.

In Luke 17:1-19, we find ten lepers who were healed by Jesus. This disease was horrific and left people isolated, for they were not allowed to be near other people. When they were healed and only one of them returned to give glory to God, Jesus asked why. The isolation that the lepers had to endure reminds me of the "social distance" requirements imposed on us during this Covid-19 pandemic. Ingratitude did not deny Christ's mercy to the nine lepers who did not give thanks; however it did deprive them of fellowship with Him. Our relationship with Him is the *most* important thing in our lives! Let's be grateful and realize that our attitude of gratitude will take us to a higher altitude. The Lord is using this to help "wake us up" and draw us closer to Him.

STAND FIRM

Many Christians have forgotten that the Christian life is not a playground, but a battlefield. As a result, very few of the Lord's people are armed, equipped, and ready to wage spiritual battle. Believe it or not, we are engaged in spiritual warfare. One of the scary things I have noticed over the years, in interactions with different people, is that we often do not accurately recognize our real enemy. The truth is that our warfare is NOT against flesh and blood.

In Ephesians 6:10-17 (NASB) we are instructed to:

> Finally, be strong in the Lord and in the strength of His might. Put on the full armor of God, so that you will be able to stand firm against the devil's schemes!

> For our struggle is not against flesh and blood, but against the rulers, against the powers, against the world forces of this darkness, against the spiritual forces of wickedness in the heavenly places. Therefore, take up the full armor of God, so that you will be able to resist in the evil day, and having done everything, to stand firm!

To stand is to make firm, to fix or establish; it's to cause a person or a thing to keep his or its place. It is the quality of one who does not hesitate and does not waver.

When Joshua crossed over into the promised land, he found many giants to destroy. However, he and Caleb stood firm in their trust in the Lord.

> Then Caleb quieted the people before Moses, and said, "Let us go up at once and take possession, for we are well able to overcome it." (Numbers 13:30).

This is an admonition to the body of Christ, the *ekklesia*, to know who and whose we are! We're to remain fixed on and certain of the Lord and His promises, no matter what "wind and waves" may arise. After this crazy pandemic subsides, a president is elected, etc. there will be other giants in the land to be defeated. For sure, the battle is the Lords (1 Sam. 17:47); however, the Lord wants to co-labor with us, His kids. It is vital that we remember, in the midst of political turmoil that has been a major area of concern this past year: Don't let the DONKEYS and the ELEPHANTS make us forget we belong to the LAMB!

> Don't let the donkeys and the elephants make us forget that we belong to the LAMB!

To be successful in our work for Jesus, to assist in the coming harvest and to help to bring heaven to earth, we must prepare to war in the Spirit and believe beyond what we see happening around us. (2 Cor. 5:7; walk by FAITH, not by sight!) Victory only comes after a battle. Be filled with great faith and expect the Lord to bring amazing and glorious days ahead. As we cross over into 2021, we will have exciting, yet challenging, choices to make. May we be willing to take off our sandals, put on the "Colossians Cloak," and stand firm!

> Eye has not seen, nor ear heard, nor have entered into the heart of man, the things which God has prepared for those who love Him. (1 Corinthians 2:9)

CURT CROOK

Curt Crook and his wife Susan accepted Christ when they were young. They traveled to the mission field after only three years of marriage. Upon returning to the United States, Curt was ordained through Grace International and in 1984, he and Susan birthed Open Door Christian Fellowship. They pastored for twenty-six years before turning leadership over to Curt's associate.

Curt has been a co-director of Revivalist School of Supernatural Ministries in Roseburg, Oregon. He has now stepped out as an entrepreneur and started a successful Fresh Salsa Business. Susan is currently a Supervisor at Douglas County, Oregon C.A.S.A.

In his business dealings and the course of daily life, Curt often sees the supernatural works of God. He continues to speak at conferences and Bible schools in the U.S. and other nations.

2
THE INVITATION
Curt Crook

We are living in a time when a world-wide pandemic and political turmoil have the potential to create and elicit the best in us. However, we must answer one important question: how shall we choose to live and navigate through these uncertain times as citizens of our nation and of this planet?

Where does God stand on the political issues of our day? What kind of line-in-the-sand does he expect us to draw? What does it mean to pick up our sword and fight our enemy? Exactly who is our enemy?

While pondering these questions, I came upon the story in Joshua 5: 13-15. Joshua's army is camped in the desert and Joshua meanders out into the expanse between his camp and Jericho, the place where the enemy is entrenched. Suddenly, there is a man "standing opposite" him with his sword drawn. Joshua steps up to the man and demands, "Are you with us or with our enemies?"

Let's pause here and take in this scene. As far as Joshua is concerned, there are only two types of people in this world: us and our enemy. Seeing an unknown figure—perhaps dressed as neither tribe—it's up to him to decide whether he should shake this guy's hand or attack him. That decision will be determined by whichever group this man sides with. "Are you for us or for them?"

"Neither," the man says.

I wonder what Joshua would do had this man not immediately identified himself as the Commander of the Army of the Lord. Would Joshua insist that he choose a side? But we will never know because Joshua falls on his face and asks for instructions. The Commander tells him to remove his sandals from his feet, because the ground on which they stand is holy.

The term holy ground is used only twice in Scripture. One reference involves Moses at the burning bush and the other reference is in this story. We can understand why Moses was told he was on holy ground. How often does one encounter a burning bush emanating the voice of God? And, although this Commander of the Army of the Lord is commonly understood to be an incarnation of the Christ, there appears to be no other reason for this ground to be holy, unless you recognize the significance of the proximity of the two warring tribes and this parcel of earth.

First, let us note that the man stands opposite Joshua. It does not say that he stands in opposition of Joshua, but opposite. Seeing one as opposite generally suggests that that person is "other than." If he is there to proclaim allegiance to one army or the other, he would be like Joshua and his enemies in that moment. But he does not come to choose a side; he appears as one who is other than Joshua—one who stands in an opposite place and position.

Have you ever had one of those times when God comes and stands opposite of where you are standing? Did you have a mindset that seemed right until the light of God illuminated its dark underbelly? That is when spiritual shifts can take place in us and our hearts expand, making room for more of His light and love.

One of my first experiences of God standing opposite me occurred when I returned from a one-year mission trip in Guatemala. My wife ran into an old school friend who was married and had a young son. The friend, Susan, shared that her little boy was being tormented every night and sometimes his covers would be yanked off his bed. My wife told her I could come over and pray. I agreed to do it, and a time was arranged.

Upon entering their home, I was introduced to Susan's husband. In that moment I was flooded with negative emotions and disturbing memories of Junior High School. Standing before me and shaking my hand was my personal bully. He didn't seem to recognize me or my name, but I thought this could be pay back for all the times he bullied me and put my head in the girl's toilets in school. I figured I did not have to pray to get rid of his son's torment; then he would know what it feels like to be helpless.

In that moment, consumed by memories created by this dad, God stood opposite me in my mind's eye. This was decision time! This was holy ground—common ground. I had a son who had been tormented after being raped at a church camp by a "minister." And now this man has a son who is tormented. He was feeling what every dad feels when he does not know what more to do. We were standing together with Jesus on holy ground—common ground. We were both young fathers. He didn't know how to pray, but I did.

> **In that moment, consumed by memories created by this dad, God stood opposite me in my mind's eye. This was decision time!**

Like the walls of Jericho, the wall of protection in my heart I had built against this man's humiliating actions came down! I gave God permission to take away all my judgements and the boyhood hatred I had carried into that moment; years of resentments, gone.

The feeling was indescribably freeing. That night the Commander of the Lord's Army took down years of anger, insecurities, emotional triggers, and so much more. He blessed me with the privilege of bringing peace to both this father and his son. To this day, I have no idea if this dad ever figured out who I was. It no longer matters to me. I am now a better human being and friend, thanks in part to moments like these.

Joshua is not standing in his camp. He is also not standing in the camp of those he believes to be his enemy. He is standing in between the camps, on common ground—the ground deemed holy by the Commander of the Army of the Lord!

In our human understanding of the military, this term translates into one thing: this guy understands warfare and planning attacks on enemies. And yet, this commander takes no sides. He isn't there to choose sides, but to stand opposite Joshua and proclaim the ground outside the two camps is holy.

I wonder sometimes, have we forgotten the gospel of peace? "Blessed are the feet of those who bring good news." Even the angels proclaim at his birth, "Peace on Earth, good will towards all men." Have we forgotten the oppositeness of our Prince of Peace? Too many of us have become people who condemn "otherness" and "oppositeness."

Doctrinal and political stances are replacing unconditional love. Do we still do unto others as we would have them do unto us? How often do we stand in the road of life with outstretched arms, waiting for the prodigals or to welcome the stranger? Do we prey on our "enemies" (think social media) instead of praying for them?

Let us not follow the mob, but rather the still small voice. God is not in the wind, the fire, or the earthquake. He is not in partisanship, positions, or votes. He stands on holy ground, unclaimed by any party, faction or group think, doctrine, sectarianism, or religious or social norms.

Here He is, in this moment, inviting you to be on His side. To do this, you must leave your position, and perhaps the position of your friends, and join with him in the opposite place. Take your shoes off; you're not going to run from this one. You must feel the commonalities between you and those you believe to be your enemies. Two different people made in his image.

Transformation takes place when we leave the ground of long-time beliefs, comfortable settings, and known outcomes, to spend time with the One who loves every human.

> "You're blessed when you care. At the moment of being 'care-full,' you'll find yourselves cared for. You're blessed when you get your inside-world, your mind and heart put right. Then you can see God in your outside world. You're blessed when you can show people how to co-operate instead of compete or fight. That's how you discover who you really are, and your place in God's family." (Matthew 5: 7-9, The Message)

Jeff McCracken

Jeff McCracken Sr. is known for his razor sharp, accurate, and sometimes humorous prophetic insight. He is also a respected apostolic voice, regionally, nationally and internationally. He has and continues to minister in many nations throughout Europe and Asia. He teaches schools on the prophetic, healing, strategic planning and more.

Jeff is a respected voice on many different boards and councils. He serves on the National Council for the US Coalition of Apostolic Leaders. He is also a published author with more books on the way.

Jeff and his wife RoxAnne are the Senior Leaders of Rainier Assembly of God in Rainier, OR, founders of the NW School of Supernatural Ministry and The Lower Columbia Healing Rooms. They have three adult children (Maddy, Ian and Abbey) and they reside in Longview, WA.

3
A NEW BEGINNING
Jeff McCracken

One is the beginning of things. It is the first of new things as well. God, of course, came before all things and is the originator of all things. I sense that we are about to step into a new normal here on the earth. A new way of life for the church, businesses, government and so much more. Not just in the United States of America but around the world. I believe that 2021, will be the beginning of a new season that God is orchestrating, but man will make come to pass on the earth.

God loves working with people to bring about His will. In Genesis 1:26-28, God tells mankind to be "fruitful and multiply." Multiplying is easy; it means having kids. But the Lord calls us to more than simply breeding. He tells us to be fruitful; He has called us to be parents. Parenting is much harder, and unfortunately far too many settle for just breeding.

Being fruitful means to bear fruit in whatever we do. We are living in what seems to be a very chaotic season, but God has been working in us, and He is taking us somewhere.

Let me explain this by identifying similar circumstances. I don't believe that Reformationist Martin Luther knew that he was at the beginning of a whole new way of thinking and that the world was about to change. He had no idea that God was using him as a change agent for events that would impact the world, altering the course of history. He was just doing the "right thing" as he was led by the Lord, having no idea his actions would create a Reformation. (We never know where our obedience will take us or how it will impact the world.) Most people that change history actually set out to just do "the right thing."

There have been many chaotic and challenging times in the world's history that gave birth to new seasons. I believe that what we are currently experiencing is possibly the greatest one.

Over the last few years, we have seen a myriad of issues rushing to compete for cultural attention that include: sexism, sexual harassment, sexual identity, capitalism versus socialism, racism, international relations, illegal behavior in government at nearly every level, environmental care and stewardship, international conspiracies, competing international accords and pressure to join them, nations challenged to live up to promises, employment/unemployment/under employment, the quality of our news and how much opinion is included, good and bad leadership, what makes good and bad leadership, abortion, partial birth abortion and full term abortion, should nations have borders, border walls, economics, healthcare, pandemics, are governors and mayors working for their people or their parties, and so much more. These concerns are not limited to America, but exist around the world. Some nations have dealt with these problems for generations.

All these issues seem to be fighting for the spotlight, demanding immediate attention. Why everything at once? The answer is that the truth is being revealed. "Revelation" means truth is revealed and no longer hidden. We tend to think that revelation uncovers something new. But revelation is not showing you something new; it is revealing something that has gone unseen. The root of the word revelation is to reveal.

Here are a couple of examples. In America, in early October 2017, multi-millionaire movie tycoon Harvey Weinstein's name suddenly appeared on the front page of newspapers with the news that he had been charged with sexual harassment. It was a revelation to most people, but it had been taking place for years. About a month later, it became more real for people when the Today show fired host Matt Lauer for sexual harassment. Many people had watched him on their television set every morning, and they trusted him. However, both men had been doing the same thing for years. The revelation came when the American public had it revealed to them and they realized what had been taking place behind closed doors. More importantly, it revealed not just the behavior, but the sad reality that such behavior was often minimized or ignored .

Suddenly there was a new normal. Actions that had been "alright" for these men, and so many others, suddenly were no longer tolerated. One week harassment was winked at by employers and the next week, lawsuits were filed. Why? These things had been wrong all along, but now God is doing something on the earth.

I am not talking about judgment, but instead a new normal. God has been preparing us "for such a time as this." The biblical book of Esther gives us the account of a courageous woman who lived through similar circumstances, and God used her to change a nation and its leadership. Esther's tale is not really a love story, but instead the story of a king who made hundreds of women perform in a contest to be his wife. Her tenacity and toughness in the face of adversity ushered in a new time in the kingdom that belonged to Queen Esther and King Artaxerxes.

> God loves working with people to bring about His will. We are living in what seems to be a very chaotic season, but God has been working in us, and He is taking us somewhere.

I prophesy that 2021 is the first year of the new normal. Everything has changed in the last couple of years and especially the past year. Government, church, business, media, entertainment, education, and family are all different than they were a year ago. God has impacted the "seven mountains." (This is a theory that all societies are impacted in seven areas: Family, Religion/Spirituality, Business [Economy and Finance], Politics [Government], Media [Communication], Arts [Entertainment, Sports, etc.], and Education.) For the record, I don't believe these comprise a biblical mandate, but they are avenues for the Kingdom to infiltrate society.

As an example, Joseph impacted the government of Egypt when he served Pharaoh. He brought the Kingdom of God into the inner sanctum of government, to a Pharaoh who did not believe in his God but nevertheless was blessed and impacted by Him. Pharaoh had a "God-experience" when Joseph interpreted his dream. Pharaoh had to know that there was a God who was interested in him personally. We need more leaders to rise in the ranks of these seven areas of society and carry the influence of the King of kings with them.

I will list each of these and share what I believe God is revealing and impacting in each arena. Please understand that these will overlap because the areas are not easy to separate. This will more clearly state what I believe God is doing instead of a broad word.

Government

God is still allowing us free will in our decisions, but I believe God is calling government to a higher standard. While President Trump is offensive to many around the world, including in the church realm, I believe that God is using him as a wrecking ball to destroy things that are fake, broken, and destructive. This is not based on President Trump's opinion of what is right and wrong, but on God's opinion of what is right and wrong. Many will say that God can't use Trump because he is so flawed. How can God use someone with so many issues and is so "crude?" If you will read through nearly any Bible

Story, it will become obvious to you that God always uses flawed people. By the way, who else is there? Everyone is flawed! Strategically, God using someone that doesn't come from the church realm actually makes it easier for Trump to be used and keeps non-believers on their heels. I also believe that God is going to have a public show of the transition and salvation of Donald Trump as President. He is also showing the church that they need to stand on the promises and prophetic words that God releases and not fold up so easily.

Look for back room deals, hidden secrets, and money schemes to be revealed and no longer tolerated. Look for conspiracies to be revealed. I believe that Hillary Clinton, President Obama, Vice President Biden, James Comey, President Bill Clinton, and many more will face consequences for their hidden and evil behavior. Some will be indicted, some will go to prison, some will mysteriously die and some will suddenly suffer from diseases. I am not saying that this is God's judgment, but I believe that as the Holy Spirit becomes more intensely present on the earth, individuals practicing such behavior will not be able to abide in His presence.

This is going to take place on several levels of government, from school boards to the highest levels in the land. God will send average people as well as anointed prophets and apostles to warn these people. He will caution them with words of knowledge that will reveal God's insight. They will be given grace and mercy and extended opportunity to do two things. First, to accept Christ and repent before Him (this will include believers that have participated in schemes, either knowingly or unknowingly). Second, I believe that those that have been involved in schemes, scams or conspiracies will have the opportunity to come clean and own their misbehavior before they are revealed. (You might ask, "Who will do the revealing, God or the devil?" To which I would respond, "Yes." The devil likes to not only get us to do the wrong thing, but he also likes to then turn on us and reveal our impropriety. Many think because it reveals sin, that it is always God. I am not as sure about who the source of revelation always is.)

Don't misunderstand—I am not claiming this to be judgment because God states that there will be ONE day of judgment, not many days. That day is yet to come, but when it does, we will all stand before His throne and answer for ourselves. However, God will allow things to be uncovered and revealed. The consequences for evil have always been in place and He will remind us. Many will reap what they have sown, and the consequences will often be dire.

> 2021 will be the first year of the new normal. Government, church, business, media, entertainment, education, and family are all different than they were a year ago.

I am looking for legalized abortion to be overturned in the United States of America. I believe that God will also be overturning other laws, rules, and mores in our culture and the various cultures of the world.

The nations of this world need to recognize that God is not only moving in the US, but He is going to impact other nations. (As I prophesy these things, I am not saying that they will all be fulfilled in 2021 but will begin in 2021 and may take a couple of years to come to fruition.)

China is going to experience some of their worst poverty and worst years of economy if they do not change their approach to human rights and international ownership rights, and decide whether or not they are willing to play well with others. Watch how China's leaders deal with Hong Kong, Macau, and others. Watch how they treat churches in their nation. God doesn't like having His kids mistreated. If human rights violations persist too long, look for China to become involved in war and be conquered (this may be governmentally but definitely economically). I say this hesitantly because I do not want to see it come to pass, but it will be up to the members of the Chinese government and how they proceed. Again, it is not judgment, but consequences.

The rest of Asia will continue seeking God and finding Him. I believe that God is going to show up in these nations and you will see and hear of them being blessed like never before. They will each worship in their own ways and in their own identities, but do not underestimate their intensity.

I believe that North and South Korea are on the verge of a revival that will impact their leaders. I have seen God dealing with Kim Jong-un. God has been warning him and talking to him through dreams and other circumstances. I believe that he is close to either accepting Christ or perhaps dying prematurely from his licentious lifestyle. If he will accept Christ, God will heal his body. I believe that God is sending messengers to him.

Watch for a major move of God in Japan. They are a stoic people that are going to come unraveled. God has so much that He wants to do through them in technology. Watch for some of the greatest inventions and cutting-edge technology to come from there for the next twenty years. Yes, they have been tech leaders for a long time, but with God onboard, they will keep their edge and launch forward in more profound ways.

I prophesy that Russia is close to a revival. If they will embrace the Lord, it will save their nation. If they turn their back on God and force their people to do the same, they will become a third-world country and be overtaken by another country. I believe that if they don't bring course correction to their nation, China or someone else will either take them over via war or by buy out. They precariously positioned and not as stable as people would think.

Europe is going to splinter and fight itself from within. They have overtly rejected Christ for too long. They will not have peace without Him. Brexit was only a beginning. Watch for infighting among the leaders of the nations (not just the top leaders but also leaders of factions within their nations). Most of this will be behind the scenes, but it will sometimes leak out and will become more fervent. The longer these nations and their people resist the Lord in a general sense, expect more infighting. They cannot have long-term peace without Jesus, Prince of Peace. I foresee factions within their nations reaching out to Christ. Some will be from churches, but because of the current changes and adjustments in the Kingdom of God that are often not being reflected in the existing churches, some of the churches will be left behind as "antiquated and powerless clubs" instead of the culturally powerful voices that they once were. A new kind of church will rise up and take their place within these nations and have a contemporary and powerful voice.

Look for African nations, tribes and people groups to come together. They have been having a move of God that is going to become more powerful than their former offenses and divisions. The seeds that Reinhard Bonnke and others sowed in that nation will begin sprouting and growing. Watch for cooperation among African nations in new ways. I also keep seeing new resources being discovered and utilized. However, where the government leaders have become rich on these in the past, I do not expect that to continue. These things will be revealed more readily. Watch this continent come into its own and go from being "the dark continent" to the "continent of light."

South America will continue its revival and will walk in the fullness of God's favor. I see Him smiling on this continent. Yes, the governmental issues will be straightened out over the next five years. There will be some godly people who will rise to lead. (These are not always going to be Christians, but like Churchill, God will use them to be fearless and bring things into order. God's order.)

The Middle East is quickly becoming sheep and goats. The recent peace accords that President Trump has brokered are revealing those that are willing to be sheep. Those that continue to fight against this will be goat nations. The goat nations will sit like spoiled children pouting that they have not got their way. They will be isolated, and time will pass them by until they become cooperative. God is putting them in "timeouts" through the passing of embargos and travel limitations.

Don't believe that God can only impact the world through Christian nations. Remember that He has spoken through a donkey before. He will use Muslim nations and other non-Christian nations to accomplish His goals. The people still need to turn to Jesus for salvation but as nations, they might be utilized by Him.

<u>Business</u>
The best new inventions, practices, ideas, processes, strategies and ways of doing business will come through revelation from God. Likewise, old processes and practices will be refined or thrown out. Look for more businesses to look to God for His insights and new revelations. I see more Christians rising to impact business with Kingdom principles. Many of these leaders will do this undercover and will not be recognized. They will be in the "secret service" of their King.

We have seen, in the last few years, that the largest entertainment company in the world (Netflix) does not own one theater. We have seen the largest transportation company (Uber) not own one vehicle. This is a time for radical change.

Watch for more accountability in tech sectors. As I am writing this, Facebook and Twitter are being called out for hiding stories and using political editing. People will get tired of this, especially in the United States. Americans will find or invent ways to not be controlled and edited. Look for other technologies to rise in communist nations. Places like China want to control people (their own and people from other nations). Their people have glimpsed freedom in the US through attending colleges and universities. Look for these people to create ways to get the "word out" through new social media platforms and other tech. Freedom was granted by God and will be pursued through man.

Media

I have heard that news media giants like CNN are realizing the errors of their ways and having to reset with different talent and a different approach to news. With so many avenues for communication, those that have tried to hide or twist the truth will become part of history like the pterodactyl. Look for big changes to happen with not just news media, but as I mentioned under the business heading, for social media and more to have a reboot or just "get the boot!"

People are growing tired of having to sift for truth and I believe that they will push for laws to help control the media. This will be a difficult endeavor since Americans feel so strongly about free speech. However, a search for fairness will likely be on the way.

Look for other nations to desire truth as well. They will begin rising up and making it known that they will not settle for "fake news" or lies from their governments, businesses, or any other sources. Truth will be re-valued.

Entertainment

I am looking for more entertainers world-wide to begin seeking Jesus. Some will do this just for show, while others will be sincere; and a third group will secretly seek Him. Those that truly seek Him will be mocked and attempts will be made to marginalize them. However, as the "Billion Soul Harvest" takes place, those who truly seek Him will have a new market that will not be so niche. (In 1975, Prophet Bob Jones received a radical prophetic word that there would be babies aborted by taking a pill, that there would be a drug called meth that would destroy people, homosexuality would come out of the closet and be celebrated in the streets and that there would be a one billion soul harvest of young people, that would take place after there are 6

> **Look for big changes to happen with not just news media, but for social media and more to have a reboot or just "get the boot!"**

billion people on the planet. We have entered into that season when there are more than a billion young people on the planet. We need to pray into this powerful word and take action through evangelism.)

These entertainers and famous people (including politicians, professional athletes, millionaires, billionaires, and other well-known leaders) will need grounded Christian leaders to mentor them. These mentors will need to be people who are not star-struck or intimidated by fame. In fact, it will distract and minimize their effectiveness if they get caught up in the hype. Instead, they need to see the person as God sees them. The potential that they carry in the Kingdom and the "gold" that is within them. Every person is created in the image of God and therefore have intrinsic value like gold. We need to see them as part of the family of God and their families as part of who they are. When we lead one person to Christ, the people that they are in relationship are likewise impacted and often drawn to salvation as well. Especially when they are prestigious.

Many of these people are tired of their flashy lives and would love to go back to their roots. If mentors can just treat them like everyone else, not be intimidated, not get money-hungry or try to use the relationship to their own benefit, then God will use them in profound ways.

Churches will need to learn how to accept well-known individuals without going crazy. These new believers will want to "taste and see and know that He is good." However, if they are distracted by people around them focusing on their fame, it will limit their ability to seek the Lord's presence.

Education
So much has changed through this COVID-19 pandemic that education is already getting a makeover. I don't think that is over. I anticipate some significant changes still to come. "Necessity is the mother of invention" and I believe that God is releasing ideas to people that will take them to the forefront. There are too many issues

with online education and people are realizing students need personal interaction. Look for ideas to come forward that will be linked with knowledge from the medical community to protect our kids.

Second, look for greater attention on the mind, will, and emotions (the soul) of students. The response to Covid will give birth for more attention being paid to the emotional health of students.

Family

Look for political correctness to die within the next ten years. This has gone too far and impacted too many areas of society. It will not have a wide scale ushering out, but it will slowly become unpopular and left behind. A new kind of respect will take its place and we need to be praying that it will be something from God. For example in Ephesians 4, we are told to "speak the truth in love." The truth without love is abuse and love without truth is enabling. But the truth in love will change lives. This is a better way to operate in life than "political correctness."

Political correctness is destroying families and I see families going back in time to rediscover some accountability (manners). The freedom of speech that has gone out of control and allowed people to yell and scream whatever they want, will be replaced with people choosing to be responsible with their language, and they will expect others to be also. This will not be an easy transition but will be fraught with battles.

There will, of course, still be those who are going to do anything to draw attention to themselves. However, the outright rudeness that has become so popular in the last few years will become tiresome to most people and it will not be so popular any longer.

Church

All these things that I have shared are somewhat dependent on mankind. I am not backing away from what I have prophesied, but I am saying that without prayer, intercession, and people willing to walk out their faith, God's desires will not be done.

There are two specific times in the New Testament that prophetic words were given, but different results came about.

First in Acts 11:27-30, we are introduced to a prophet named Agabus and he correctly prophesied a famine that would take place. The disciples, in response to the prophetic word, sent relief for the people.

The same prophet, in Acts 21:10-11, prophesies over Paul.

> And as we stayed many days, a certain prophet named Agabus came down from Judea. When he had come to us, he took Paul's belt, bound his own hands and feet, and said, "Thus says the Holy Spirit, 'So shall the Jews at Jerusalem bind the man who owns this belt, and deliver him into the hands of the Gentiles.' "

In reality, the Gentiles rescued Paul from the Jews.

> He immediately took soldiers and centurions, and ran down to them. And when they saw the commander and the soldiers, they stopped beating Paul. Then the commander came near and took him, and commanded him to be bound with two chains; and he asked who he was and what he had done.
> (Acts 21:32-33)

The commander handed Paul over to the Jews, which was the exact opposite of what was prophesied. Acts 22:30-

The next day, because he wanted to know for certain why he was accused by the Jews, he released him from his bonds, and commanded the chief priests and all their council to appear, and brought Paul down and set him before them.

The point is that we see through a glass darkly. The prophets of the New Testament weren't always exactly correct, yet they were NOT stoned to death, because they no longer lived in the Old Testament.

The Apostle Paul, writer of most of the New Testament, missed a prophetic word as well.

> "Men, I perceive that this voyage will end with disaster and much loss, not only of the cargo and ship, but also our lives." (Acts 27:10)

Later in the chapter, there is no loss of life, which might seem like a minor detail, unless you were on the ship!

> "And now I urge you to take heart, for there will be no loss of life among you, but only of the ship. For there stood by me this night an angel of the God to whom I belong and whom I serve..." (Vs. 22-23)

Paul misses this prophetic word, but we do not tear his writings from the Bible. My point is, let us be filled with grace and understand that these prophetic words are received in prayer, and they require prayer and cooperative people to come to pass.

God's will shall come to pass, but the timing often depends on our cooperation with Him. We need to hear God's voice and then act, leaning in through prayer to see His will done on earth.

GEORGE WATKINS

Dr. George Watkins is an apostle and prophet and is director of Faith Producers Ministries. He has been holding crusades and leadership seminars and helping to establish churches throughout the world for over fifty years. His teaching includes radio broadcasting, audio and video messages, and a Bible correspondence course. He is also the author of several books.

Dr. Watkins loves to minister to the local church, has a heart for pastors, and is a seasoned veteran, having pastored his last church for twenty-nine years. He believes that God means what He says, that His Word applies to our everyday lives, and that it has power to make us whole in mind, body, and soul.

George and his wife Arlis live in Mount Vernon, WA and are the parents of three adult children: Tony, Tiffany, Corbin, and their families.

POURING WATER ON THE SACRIFICE
Dr. George Watkins

"God is the slowest person you'll ever meet, but He's always on time."

Fred Hall was one of my early mentors. He was a contemporary of my father; they were both young preachers together in the early Pentecostal movement in Southern California. Not too many miles—and years—away from that great outpouring at Azusa Street in Los Angeles, California, my father and Fred were raised up in the fire of that impacting spiritual event. Fred was a transplanted Texan with all the stories to prove it. Raised on the plains of Texas, he learned the rough-and-tumble life of those early days just after the turn of the century. When Fred got saved, God took that rugged nature that God had given him and anointed it. He then became a noted evangelist. In great gospel tents and large auditoriums all over our nation, he conducted healing revivals in the 1950s and 60s.

God sent Fred to Washington, D.C. to open up a revival center with services every night, and when I took my first evangelistic trip to the East Coast I had the privilege of conducting a number of meetings in the church that Fred had established. It was during those times I learned a level of prayer that I had not experienced before. You see, Fred Hall was not just an evangelist; his greatest gift was his prayer ministry and the intercession that God had given him for our nation's capital. Many of the services and most of the sermons I preached are a dim memory by now, but what is still crystal clear are the times we laid on the floor together and prayed far into the night.

Those days, I was in a season of trying to find the direction that God had for me. How was my gift to fit into the body of Christ? I asked many questions while we were together, and we prayed about some of them. One night after we had finished praying, Fred said, "George, you know God is the slowest person you'll ever meet, but He's always on time."

I had no idea at the time how much that phrase would impact my entire life as I reflected on it time and again. Most of those reflections happened during periods in my life where I was stretched or pressed and needed an answer from the Lord. You know what I mean; you've been there. You pray, you wait, you fast, you seek, you ask. And if we are honest, we are tempted to beg God for something, anything; show yourself, Lord!

Then I would remember what Fred Hall told me those years ago. "George, He may be slow, but He's always on time." With that statement comes a kaleidoscope of biblical images of men and women who have been memorialized in the Scriptures for their faith in God, their steadfastness, and their determination to stand strong until the answer came.

For those of us who were raised in the church, the gang from Hebrews 11 is part of our family tree. We talked about them at the dinner table and heard the pastor preach about them often throughout the year. Sacrifice, standing on the Word of God, going the extra mile, doing without so we could spread the gospel. These were all common in those days of early pioneering and establishing churches and places of worship throughout the nation.

If you are not someone who takes notes of your activities and your thoughts, then you'll probably suffer from the common human weakness of selective memory. Depending on our character foundation, we either remember all the good times or all the bad times. Someone may ask us what kind of meeting we had. Was it a good one? We answer yes; the glory of God was there. And I was anointed as I preached and had many healings and salvations.

However, what is left out is the preparation and the journey that got us to that glorious meeting. There were times of doubt, fear, anxiety, and wondering if God was going to show up again. How do I know that? Because it is the most common attack the enemy has to assault those who are walking in God's purposes and will.

These challenges are really the glory times. The meetings themselves are just the overflow of the victories that we have won in prayer with those encounters that we had face-to-face with the Father. Times like that can only happen because we know that the Father may be slow, but He's never late.

In First Peter 1:7, Peter describes what I call "Golden Christians." These are the ones who have gone through tests without being run off by the enemy's threats and intimidation. Peter teaches us that the trying of our faith is more precious than gold. More valuable and of greater worth than a pile of gold is the one who has not panicked or run away in the face of a trial.

A few days ago, God dropped some nuggets in my spirit about the times that we are in. He said, "Before you enter into your trial, I have already prepared your exit." Think about that and remember that he is always on time. He is never surprised by your trial, or even your mistakes and failures.

And He has promised us that He would never fail us or forsake us.

So we stand together at the start of a new year and look around at our circumstances and listen to our friends and our society and we wonder again: is God going to show up on time? Perhaps you've never gone through those questions. Lord, I know you were here tonight, but will you show up tomorrow night?

In reference to that I am reminded of Kathryn Kuhlman who was one of the great spiritual generals of the last century. God raised her up in a time when the nation needed to see the power and the magnificent wonder of God's healing sick bodies and bringing people into the kingdom of God.

Reverend Kuhlman conducted mass healing meetings for several decades, across our nation, in large auditoriums with undeniable miracles night after night.

> "Golden Christians" are those who have gone through tests without being run off by the enemy's threats and intimidation. Peter teaches us that the trying of our faith is more precious than gold.

Yet I've heard it said of Kathryn Kuhlman that she would pray behind the curtain before the service started, walking back and forth calling on the Holy Spirit. Will you be here tonight? Will you come again? Oh, Holy Spirit, don't forsake me now.

Again, to encourage you in the struggle of faith that you may be in regarding something in your personal life or in the outcome of our national elections and the future of our nation. Let me remind you of the greatest prophet that ever lived: John the Baptist. Most of us know that he was Jesus's cousin, and was conceived in a miraculous way, and was the opening act for Jesus's appearance and presentation to the world. How can we forget that great scene the Scriptures recount as John was baptizing people in the Jordan River, and Jesus approached him. John declared "Behold the Lamb of God takes away the sins of the world." Then the Holy Spirit settled on Jesus as gentle as a dove, and the voice of the Father spoke, "This is my beloved son."

John was granted the incredible honor of baptizing Jesus, and the Lord called him the greatest prophet that ever lived.

Then take a snapshot of John the Baptist's disciples coming to Jesus and asking the question. "Are you the one we're looking for, or is there another coming?" John the Baptist was in prison. He was about to give his life for the Kingdom and for the mission that God had given him. And he had a doubt. Did I really see and hear clearly that he is the Christ? So doubt comes to us all. But remember this. God may be slow, but He's never late.

I love the testimony that Jesus sent back to John when He answered the disciples. "Go your way, and tell John what things you have seen and heard; how that the blind see, the lame walk, the lepers are cleansed, the deaf hear, the dead are raised, to the poor of the gospel is preached." Jesus was describing to John the fruits of His ministry in real-time. John had entered in by faith to a journey that the Father had given him, not knowing the exit. Jesus was manifesting to him what the exit looked like for his journey.

Reflect for a moment on the cloud of witnesses that are referred to in Hebrews 12. These are the ones mentioned in the "Hall of Faith" in Hebrews 11. Each of them entered a journey and a destiny that God laid before them. Men and women who shaped history and gave their lives for the purposes of God's Kingdom. Some of them performed miracles; others delivered multitudes out of bondage. Yet the Scriptures tell us they died in faith, believing that their journey would be completed by you and me as we live out our journey.

Pay close attention to Hebrews 11:39 and 40.

> And all these, having gained approval through their faith, did not receive what was promised because God had provided something better for us so that apart from us, they should not be made perfect.

You and I are working and laboring in a Kingdom that will never end—the Kingdom of God. However, we are not only laboring to gain a better future. We are also reaching back to the saints of old, completing their journey. I am convinced that the departed saints that Paul calls the cloud of witnesses are not only cheering us on but laboring together with us. What they didn't fulfill in their journey is completed in ours.

However, this means that our lives will never really be complete because the next generation of Kingdom soldiers will go on to fulfill the promise of what we believed and hoped for, but never saw the fruit completely manifested. This, my friends, is life in the Kingdom of God.

So, we stand at this point of history looking into a new year and asking the Father for insight and direction. We asked the prophets, "What are you seeing and what are you hearing? Give us some encouragement, give us some hope that God will not fail us in this season of our journey."

We stand as people in a tension between the past and the future. We know that we cannot fail because God has promised us, according to Daniel's prophecy, that the Kingdom that we are involved in will swell and fill the whole earth. A portion of the body of Christ puts most of this off for some future event, something that will happen after the end of time. It is my conviction that these promises that God has given us are unfolding now as we walk out his purposes on earth, and they will happen in real-time, with real people. We will witness the unfolding that God has planned for His Kindom even in this new year. But do not expect to see the fulness of the Kingdom in your lifetime. Because, like the saints before us, we will pass our baton to the next generation.

"OK, preacher, come back down to earth now. Don't you know we're in real trouble? Our nation is in chaos; we are divided over political differences, and we have a President that has been anointed of God to lead us for another four years. Meanwhile, others are trying to steal the election by deceitful actions."

Yes, I get it. But let me tell you what the Spirit of God is dropping in my spirit. It is the title of this chapter I'm writing.

"Pouring water on the sacrifice."

Why in the world would Elijah pour water over the sacrifice that he is about ready to ask God to consume with fire? He is a key player in the middle of a national crisis. What happens on that mountain is going to determine the future of Israel. God has placed him there as a prophet. The false prophets are standing around, watching to see what his God is going to do. They are calling on their gods, cutting themselves, and begging their gods to come and prove themselves by burning up their sacrifice.

Elijah doesn't want to just win this contest; he wants to blow the false prophets out of the water. He wants to take the people's breath away. What he really wants to do is break the back of the enemy for good. If we are going to win the battle that we are in, let's not just squeak through a win, but let's have a landslide win.

So Elijah calls for the water pots. Pour it on, boys, he says. Again and again, the water is poured over the sacrifice until it runs into the ditch that was dug around it—filling it up. Then he calls upon the name of God to send the fire. Now pay attention to the magnitude of the victory that God is about ready to give him.

Note, the country Elijah is in is a dry country. Fire can start easily. So he gets the sacrifice so soaked with water that only a miracle could consume it. Look what God did. He burnt the sacrifice and licked up all the water around it.

> You and I are working and laboring in a Kingdom that will never end. We are also reaching back to the saints of old, completing their journey.

A few weeks ago, the Spirit dropped this in my spirit: "I'm going to take the wheels off their chariots." Of course, I instantly remembered the miracle deliverance the children of Israel experienced while they were in the middle of passing through the water on dry ground. That's when the Egyptian army showed up. Pharaoh had come out of his stupor and realized he was losing his slave population, so he went after them with his army to haul them back to Egypt. Remember, this was the greatest army in the world at that time. Pharaoh and the soldiers showed up at the water's edge as the children of Israel were getting across to the other side.

Now put yourself in their place and imagine the terror and fear that could have come upon someone when they saw that great army show up. Perhaps you may be feeling something similar at this moment, as we look into this new year and see the spiritual armies around us that are against the church and our Christ. We hear voices on every level, telling us that we are going to fail and be destroyed. This is not just a national issue because of the election that is being challenged concerning suspected cheating; this is a righteousness issue. Because of that, God is involved in it, and when God is involved, we know the end is always planned. And that plan is always victory.

We know what happened. God sent His angels and took the wheels off the Egyptians' chariots, and that army drowned in the water that rushed back into place, just as the children of Israel stepped out on the other side. I'm telling you, my friends, this next year is going to be a time of "wheels coming off the chariots" of those that have come against the church of Jesus, our nation, and our righteous cause in this Earth.

In a trial or test, remember this: the exit is always planned before the entrance happens. God never says, "Whoops; I sure missed that one." The Scriptures tell us that He knows the end from the beginning.

So, pour water on the sacrifice. Get it good and wet, so the miracle will really be magnificent. Today's challenge that we are in as a nation, church, and family are all tied to the miracles of deliverance that God has prepared for us this coming year. Do you know how I know that? Because there's a whole lot of water being poured on our head right now, and sometimes we feel soaked to the skin.

I love the Scripture that says, "God won't give us something that will break us, but in every way, He will make a way of escape."

So, we prepare for the fire, and we get water. We ask God for a victory, and we get a battle. We believe for church growth, and the government shuts the church down. I call that water on the sacrifice.

Why would God allow us to enter a time of testing like this? To produce "Golden Christians," that's why. Men and women of faith who have been through a fiery trial so that their faith becomes more precious than gold.

Remember what Fred Hall told me. "God is the slowest person you'll ever know, but He's always on time." You and I live by a calendar and a clock. God does not live by our calendar nor our clock, but He does operate according to His schedule. And you know what? He's got a better grasp of time than we have because He is never late. He's always on time.

What does it mean to you when you hear the phrase "God is going to take the wheels off the chariots"? My prophetic sense is that He is going to expose evil plots. This is already being evidenced by the discovery of dishonesty and downright criminal activity in the United States' election.

> **Pour water on the sacrifice. Get it good and wet, so the miracle will really be magnificent.**

I believe God is going to take the wheels off the chariots of those who involved themselves in such activities.

There are hidden agendas in our political system that have been hidden, but God is going to yank the covers off of them. Plans that the enemy has been putting together for years are going to be discovered and taken apart. Some governors and mayors in our states and cities are going to be removed from office in these coming months and years. God is going to take the wheels off their chariots.

The wheels of the chariots will be taken off the demonic viruses and sicknesses that have been launched against our nation and the nations of the world. Even though we understand that the virus came from China, it really came from the evil one, the devil, because he is behind all these diseases that would take our lives. God is taking the wheels off their chariots.

Is the storm over? Is the contest through? Has the test been completed?

No. As long as we're on this earth, there will be contests that we engage in, and there will be victories that we will win.

I heard someone say recently, "Mountain tops are there to point out the valleys."

So here's my word for the coming year.

Stand strong among the prophets of baal and call down fire upon the sacrifice in this coming year.

Believe that God will show up on time, every time, because His promises never fail.

Remember that you are working with the cloud of witnesses and you are completing their task in your journey of faith. And your walk of faith will be completed by the disciples that you produce in these coming days.

Keep in mind as we enter this new year that you hold the future in your heart; it's that prophetic vision that was put there by the Word of God. The expression of that vision is formed by your mouth as you speak it forth and declare it to be. In the Kingdom of God, we are really the architects of our own destiny and future.

Paul said in Second Corinthians 12 that we all should prophesy. He also wrote in the 10th chapter of Romans that the Word of God was in our mouth; and that Word was given by the preaching of the good news of the Kingdom of God. That Word connected with faith in the heart will produce what the Bible calls salvation. The word for salvation means to be saved, delivered, healed, and made whole. It is really the voice of prophecy coming out of your mouth because of the Word of God in your heart, producing faith.

So let's stand together as a company of believers and launch our prophetic salvos and prayers over the walls of the enemies fortress into next year. Together we claim and declare a righteous victory in our political life as a nation. We claim and declare an end to child sacrifice in our nation. We claim and declare that this nation that we live in and the states where we have our homes will embrace the principles of the Kingdom of God on earth. We agree together as the body of Christ—both those who have gone on before and those who are still on the earth—that the Kingdom of God will increase, like the rock in Daniel's prophecy, and fill the whole earth.

We stand together as saints of God and declare that the church of Jesus Christ will have a revelation of who the Father is and will have a face-to-face relationship that alters the way we function. This will change the world around us.

This is the year for mass salvations, not only for this nation but for the nations of the world. It is time for God to bring His family back to Himself. Together we call in the backslider. We declare that the brokenhearted and those who have been disappointed by life will be drawn into the Lord's loving arms and tender mercies and be healed. We speak a unifying of church bodies that will work together in concert to see their cities changed into communities of Kingdom Living.

We prophesy that the angelic will be increased in our midst, and the body of Christ will gain deeper revelation and understanding of who angels are and how they function among us. We can then work with them to see the victory God has planned for us.

We prophesy that the heavens will be opened just as "Jacob's ladder" shows us the example. Angels are ascending and descending, bringing blessings and miracles from Heaven and taking messages back to the Father.

We believe together as men and women of the Kingdom of God for an increase of the gifts of the Spirit so that members in the body of Christ will understand their personal ministries, and will rise up and do the work of the ministry according to Ephesians 4:11.

The Scriptures tell us it is God's desire and purpose that all men be saved and come to the knowledge of the truth. We prophesy as a united body of Christ that these words that God has given will come to pass in our generation.

Oh God, I pray that a manifestation of your Kingdom will continue to be revealed in these days ahead of us. I pray that the body of Christ will have a revelation of their ability to go into the heavenlies by faith and sit before the Father, listening to His counsel. I pray that we will have a continued revelation of the cloud of witnesses that are around us, knowing that we are fulfilling their journey as we walk into ours.

> Believe that God will show up on time, every time, because His promises never fail.

Oh, Father, remove the wheels from the chariots of the enemy. Expose the dark secrets and the plans that the enemy has put into the hearts of men and women who are trying to lead our nation astray. Father, exalt your church, exalt those who are leading the church, exalt your people in the church to the proper position in Jesus name.

I pray that this new year 2021 will be a time of outpouring in a way we've only imagined and prayed for. We dream of having another Azuza Street. We remember the Hebrides Islands revival and the miracles that happened at that season of outpouring. We think of the outpouring of your Spirit in Wales, and how great that outpouring was; so powerful that 100,000 people came to know you and changed the course of their history.

We remember the mystics and the saints of old that shook nations and made a difference in their day; and we say, oh Lord bring it again. Those men of old, how they stepped into villages and towns that were filled with sickness, and the entire town was healed instantly as their feet touched the ground. These are our dreams of faith and prayers that this coming year will be a year of harvest. Lord, bring the harvest in from the seeds that have been planted and watered by your believing church. May 2021 be the greatest year the church has experienced. It's miracle time—a time of heaven on earth.

Hear our prayers, Lord. Your children are calling the Father and believing for an answer. For you told us that while we were speaking, you hear us, and before we are through the answers on the way.

We know you are never late; you're always on time.

We believe you know how to take the wheels off the chariots and dismantle the plans of the enemy.

We know there has been water poured on the sacrifice, and today we are calling fire to fall upon that sacrifice this coming year, believing that God is going to show Himself strong to those who put their trust in the Lord.

You told us that we could ask largely, and today we do. We do it because we are in your name; therefore, we have the authority of your name, and we release these requests, commands, directions of prayer, judgments, and freedom for this new year we face.

In Jesus's name.

HERB MARKS

Herb Marks prayed the sinner's prayer on his knees under a streetlight at 4:00 AM in August 1971. Moments later he experienced hearing tens of thousands of angels worshiping God. This encounter marked his life to this day.

A few years later he and others began a ministry for youth called "Sought Out." They focused on presentation of the Word with signs following. The ministry grew to include attendees from seventy-two churches representing eleven denominations.

Herb is an associate pastor at Sonrise Christian Center located in Everett, Washington. He oversees the House of Prayer where many miraculous answers to prayer have been recorded.

Herb has been married to Bethany for twenty-seven years. They have a twenty-one-year-old son named Deryck.

5
TELL THEM "THERE IS A FUTURE!"
Herb Marks

A Heavenly Encounter

I was praying in the Spirit in the living room of our home, enjoying the unction that accompanies praying loudly, the sound like no other on this planet: the heavenly language given by the precious Holy Spirit to His people.

I stood peering from the kitchen island into the living room, praying aloud, when I began to experience the presence of God. The hairs on my arms stood on end with a swirling sense of heaven invading our home. The room was becoming bright with an Illuminating mist suspended in the air. Chills ran down my back. I was immediately aware of an area in my life in need of repentance. I dropped to my knees and corrected my heart. The Lord required an area of me and I gave it. I stayed on my knees until He was done. His presence then saturated our living room.

I looked deeper into the bright mist and saw movement of fuzzy, undefined shapes moving about. I stood to my feet with a sense of weighty awe as I respectfully watched. The shapes quickly became clearer. Filling our home was the buzz of Kingdom business. The shapes in the bright essence were messengers doing the bidding of God. Angels were on task—smooth, confident, and not at all hurried.

They were focused, but not pressed. The Lord gave them assignments, and off they went to perform them.

Then I noticed to the far left a man standing in the luminance. He was the one administrating assignments to the Angels. The bright mist was around him and upon him; it was not coming from within him. I knew he was not Deity. I asked the Lord who this person was, and He revealed to me that it was Moses.

The one directing and sending the angels was Moses. He suddenly stopped and looked at me. This commanding individual with his bright, tightly woven beard was looking squarely at me. In perfect unison, all activity paused in the room. It was as if the walls had disappeared. I was taken aback. I froze, auditing my behavior and actions to be sure I honored this moment. Certainly, I did not want to say something I would regret later. I stood like a stone statue. He then said these words verbatim, "Tell them there is a future. God will have His way."

In other words, He's got this. Moses then went back to dispersing assignments to the messengers going about Kingdom business on the earth.

There is a future. Tell them. How am I to tell you?

Jesus said there was only one thing necessary (Luke 10:42). Scripture mentions it only once this way, and it is here. Mary sat as at Jesus' feet and Mary's sister, Martha, did not. Martha was busy. Jesus told Martha that what Mary was doing was better, in fact necessary; it was required.

What Jesus said in that moment was necessary. Mary was receiving Jesus' counsel and it was necessary to move into the future. Oh, that we would do the same. If ever there was a time to embrace the counsel of Jesus it is now.

Will you do what is necessary? Some say the reason we don't pray as we could is that we think we can do it ourselves. This kind of "prayer delay" shapes a kingdom cultural deficit we learn to live with in our hearts. Many have learned to live with a deficit of prayer. It's frightening to consider the predominant sound in their prayerless soul is themselves!

I have met with and prayed with folks in approximately 3,000 prayer counseling sessions. I learned early that a moment in His presence does more than hours of counseling! Our chief intention during these sessions was to enter His presence and hear what He was saying for this person's life. We were seeking His counsel. Jesus' perspective is remarkable, and often different from ours. Not only what He says, but even the way He says it has power to align a person's outlook and motivations correctly.

There's a pastor in our great state of Washington who shared how his counseling load noticeably dropped when he started requiring folks to go into the church's sanctuary and seek God one hour prior to meeting with him. He was asking them to first take time to sit at Jesus' feet before meeting with him and the results were profound! Many even left without seeing this pastor because their answer came in that hour. Jesus is our counselor. He is all-wise and He is closer than a friend! Jesus' counsel is necessary.

 Mary was on point! How did Mary become the one to pour oil on Jesus' feet as a prophetic gesture pointing to Jesus' burial? The oil was worth a year's wages (Luke 7:36-50). How is it that her actions triggered Judas into the ultimate betrayal? This passion enabled her to honor and demonstrate His Kingship publicly. Having a crucial role in these precise moments, these game-changing moments, came from being in step with Jesus' cadence, His timing.

Mary probably didn't notice anyone else in the room at that moment. It was just her and her King as she gave Him a valuable gift. It was simply Mary giving of her highest value to Jesus. How did she come to express, and have providence usher her into, this tremendous exhibit between God and a redeemed love?

We must go back to Mary sitting at His feet. This is our example of what is necessary for intimacy with our King and Savior. Mary immersed herself in the counsel of Jesus. It changed her. She began to engage His thoughts, and her perception was altered and redeveloped. She was changed. Because of this paradigm shift within her whole existence, she found herself in step with—catapulted into—her future.

"Tell Them There Is A Future!"
You will know what it is as you sit at His feet and receive His counsel. Take time to understand His wise counsel for this hour. We need His counsel during this unprecedented time we are facing in our personal lives, as a church, and as a nation.

Please allow me this last point. I am disturbed at the upsurge of talking heads claiming to have insight for your decision-making, attempting to be your guides. Social media is log jammed with myriads of opinions and conclusions.

Some say another type of terrorist that has infiltrated America is the newscaster. The proliferation of pandemic information shared without hope has placed this country on its ear. Anxiety and fear have gripped Americans. A narrative that death is literally in the air has been extensively and relentlessly proclaimed. Americans have never grappled with this weighty inertia of concern for their personhood and loved ones. "We don't know what to think because we don't know who or what is accurate anymore" is common dialogue.

Most people would agree: "We just don't know enough about this pandemic. We have even heard there could be a darker agenda behind it all. But one thing we do know is it can kill you."

Be careful of the many siren voices. The voices that keep shifting and casting an atmosphere of uncertainty and fear. They are like the prophets of Baal. Speaking as experts. As if they know what they are talking about. Certain and full of confidence. But often their reports are misleading and outcome is dire.

King Ahab was surrounded with 400 voices that were not speaking accurately and the king allowed it (2 Chronicles 18). Jehoshaphat asked Ahab if he knew of a prophetic voice who spoke truth. Ahab kept one voice of truth in prison, so Jehoshaphat asked Ahab to call for him: the prophet Micaiah. After being threatened by the other false prophets to echo their rhetoric, Micaiah delivered truth to Ahab. Because Ahab did not want truth, he sent Micaiah back to prison with bread and water rations. Ahab followed his own agenda. He chose not to honor God nor obey His laws. Ahab only served himself and raised up 400 voices to support his rebellion. His unwillingness to listen to God's truth cost Ahab his life.

It will cost us too! If you don't want truth you won't have it. If you ignore, delay, or imprison truth, it will cost you. Truth is not a thing, it's a person! Jesus said, "I am the way the truth and the life." Your posture and your focus are not horizontal, but vertical. "I lift up my eyes to you, to you whose throne is in heaven" (Psalm 123:1).

> We must go back to Mary sitting at His feet. This is our example of intimacy with our King and Savior. Mary immersed herself in the counsel of Jesus.

Loved ones, "There is a Future." Go be with Jesus, sit at His feet. This is necessary for you to perceive His future for your life. It is probable things will not be exactly the same when we come to the other side of this pandemic. In Jesus we will be strong. It may not be easy, but it will be profound because we will be closer to Him, operating in the power of His counsel.

Now go sit at His feet.

Dan Hammer

Dr. Dan C. Hammer is a servant-leader and visionary with a passion to reach the unloved with the gospel of Jesus Christ. Dr. Hammer is committed to intercessory prayer and uncovering the gifts of the Holy Spirit in the lives of believers. He regularly teaches how to attain life's full potential by understanding God's purpose. He is the president of Seattle Bible College and has taught there since 1984. He is a member of the United States Coalition of Apostolic Leaders, and he heads up SEND—Sonrise Equipping Network Development.

Dan has traveled and ministered in thirty-seven nations. He has a Bachelor of Theology from Seattle Bible College and a Master's and Doctorate from Bakke Graduate University. In 1986, Dan and his wife Terry planted Sonrise Christian Center as an independent Fellowship of Christian Assemblies in Everett, Washington, where they continue to serve as senior apostolic leaders. They have three adult children and six grandchildren.

FIVE KEYS FOR 2021
Dr. Dan Hammer

As we look at 2021 approaching us, after all the surprises of 2020, it is vital that we keep our eyes on the Lord by being in prayer and being in His Word. I sense the Lord has given me two Scripture portions important for the coming year. God wants to quicken His Word to our hearts in 2021 as we draw near to Him in intimacy.

The first Scripture the Lord spoke to me for 2021 was:

> But you, beloved, building yourselves up on your most holy faith, praying in the Holy Spirit, keep yourselves in the love of God, looking for the mercy of our Lord Jesus Christ unto eternal life. And on some have compassion, making a distinction; but others save with fear, pulling them out of the fire, hating even the garment defiled by the flesh.
> Now to Him who is able to keep you from stumbling,
> And to present you faultless
> Before the presence of His glory with exceeding joy,
> To God our Savior,
> Who alone is wise,
> Be glory and majesty,
> Dominion and power,
> Both now and forever.
> Amen. (Jude 20-25)

As we look at the context of these verses, we see Jude is talking about the last days. Jude tells us we are going to have to "earnestly contend for the faith that was once delivered to the saints." The church is going to be facing more opposition from the enemy in 2021! I believe we can expect more persecution coming our way this year. Ungodly people will deny the Lord Jesus Christ and come against Him and the people of God. Jude reminded us to remember the words of the apostles of Jesus Christ in the last days, that mockers would come who would walk in ungodly lusts and cause divisions. Jude said these people will not have the Spirit. These warnings are for us!

So according to Jude 20 we are to be praying in the Spirit and building ourselves up in the most holy faith. I believe we need to be praying in tongues more than we ever have in our lives. As we activate our prayer language, we get built up in our faith against the evil one and his minions.

Paul, the apostle, gave us instruction in the first letter to the church at Corinth, about using our personal prayer language.

> Pursue love, and desire spiritual gifts, but especially that you may prophesy. For he who speaks in a tongue does not speak to men but to God, for no one understands him; however, in the spirit he speaks mysteries. But he who prophesies speaks edification and exhortation and comfort to men. He who speaks in a tongue edifies himself, but he who prophesies edifies the church. I wish you all spoke with tongues, but even more that you prophesied; for he who prophesies is greater than he who speaks with tongues, unless indeed he interprets, that the church may receive edification.
> (1 Corinthians 14:1-5)

According to this passage, when we pray in tongues we edify ourselves. This will be a year when we need to build ourselves up in the Lord. Paul prayed in tongues frequently.

> I thank my God I speak with tongues more than you all; yet in the church I would rather speak five words with my understanding, that I may teach others also, than ten thousand words in a tongue.
> (1 Corinthians 14:18-19)

In Jude 20 we are told to keep ourselves in the love of God. As well as praying in tongues we need to do this also. This is the second key. How do we keep ourselves in the love of God? We receive God's love. One of the ways we receive God's love is to forgive ourselves. John, the apostle, tells us

> For God so loved the world that He gave His only begotten Son, that whoever believes in Him should not perish but have everlasting life. For God did not send His Son into the world to condemn the world, but that the world through Him might be saved.
> (John 3:16-17)

God saves us from our sins and we can know His forgiveness and keep ourselves in the love of God. If we do not receive forgiveness from God and forgive ourselves, we do not let God love us. Let God love you! Forgive yourself.

1 John 3:1-3 states,

> Behold what manner of love the Father has bestowed on us, that we should be called children of God! Therefore the world does not know us, because it did not know Him. Beloved, now we are children of God; and it has not yet been revealed what we shall be, but we know that when He is revealed, we shall be like Him, for we shall see Him as He is. And everyone who has this hope in Him purifies himself, just as He is pure.

We keep ourselves in the love of God by knowing we are God's children—sons and daughters of the heavenly Father! That is the love that has been bestowed upon us. This causes us to purify ourselves because we want to be like our Father in heaven! The world does not know us, but our Father in heaven does know us. I encourage you to begin every morning in 2021 by receiving the love of the Father, Son, and Holy Spirit.

We keep ourselves in the love of God by loving other believers.

> "A new commandment I give to you, that you love one another; as I have loved you, that you also love one another. By this all will know that you are My disciples, if you have love for one another." (John 13:34-35)

God is bringing us into oneness of heart and encouraging us to love one another like Jesus has loved us. This is how people will know that we are His disciples. Our love for each other needs to be shown in practical ways.

> By this we know love, because He laid down His life for us. And we also ought to lay down our lives for the brethren. But whoever has this world's goods, and sees his brother in need, and shuts up his heart from him, how does the love of God abide in him? My little children, let us not love in word or in tongue, but in deed and in truth. (1 John 3:16-18)

This will be a year to let God's love mature in us.

> No one has seen God at any time. If we love one another, God abides in us, and His love has been perfected in us. (1 John 4:12)

2021 will give us opportunities to keep ourselves in the love of God. God wants His body to dwell in oneness and unity.

The second passage of Scripture that God gave me for 2021 is:

> Watch, stand fast in the faith, be brave, be strong. Let all that you do be done with love. I urge you, brethren—you know the household of Stephanas, that it is the firstfruits of Achaia, and that they have devoted themselves to the ministry of the saints— that you also submit to such, and to everyone who works and labors with us. I am glad about the coming of Stephanas, Fortunatus, and Achaicus, for what was lacking on your part they supplied. For they refreshed my spirit and yours. Therefore acknowledge such men.
> (1 Corinthians 16:13-18)

There are five keys in this passage: Watch, stand fast in the faith, be brave, be strong, and let everything be done in love. Let's look at them individually.

Watch

We need to watch in 2021 to see what God is doing. Not what we want God to do, but what God is doing. This was the principle Jesus lived by on earth.

> Then Jesus answered and said to them, "Most assuredly, I say to you, the Son can do nothing of Himself, but what He sees the Father do; for whatever He does, the Son also does in like manner. For the Father loves the Son, and shows Him all things that He Himself does; and He will show Him greater works than these, that you may marvel." (John 5:19-20)

Like Jesus we should be looking and watching for what the Father is doing. "Watch" means to be on the alert.

> "Watch therefore, for you know neither the day nor the hour in which the Son of Man is coming."
> (Matthew 25:13)

We are to be watching for His coming and watching where He is moving around us. A soldier of Jesus Christ should always be alert and on watch. Be on guard against the enemy of your soul.

Stand fast in the faith
This is the faith that causes us to stand on God's word and His will. We need to stand for the Word of God and its truths. Keep yourselves standing on the rock of Christ's teachings.

> "But why do you call Me 'Lord, Lord,' and not do the things which I say? Whoever comes to Me, and hears My sayings and does them, I will show you whom he is like: He is like a man building a house, who dug deep and laid the foundation on the rock. And when the flood arose, the stream beat vehemently against that house, and could not shake it, for it was founded on the rock. But he who heard and did nothing is like a man who built a house on the earth without a foundation, against which the stream beat vehemently; and immediately it fell. And the ruin of that house was great."
> (Luke 6:46-49)

Jesus used the Word of God when the devil tempted Him in the wilderness. This should be our strategy too. STAND!

Third, be brave!
God told this to Joshua as he went into the promised land.

> "Only be strong and very courageous, that you may observe to do according to all the law which Moses My servant commanded you; do not turn from it to the right hand or to the left, that you may prosper wherever you go. This Book of the Law shall not depart from your mouth, but you shall meditate in it day and night, that you may observe to do according to all that is written in it. For then you will make your way prosperous, and then

> you will have good success. Have I not commanded you? Be strong and of good courage; do not be afraid, nor be dismayed, for the LORD your God is with you wherever you go." (Joshua 1:7-9)

The enemy will try to use fear as a weapon in this year. We can be strong and courageous. We can defeat the enemy in Jesus's Name. God is raising up a brave group of warriors for this last days' battle. We need to put on the whole armor of God and take it up in the fight.

> Finally, my brethren, be strong in the Lord and in the power of His might. Put on the whole armor of God, that you may be able to stand against the wiles of the devil. For we do not wrestle against flesh and blood, but against principalities, against powers, against the rulers of the darkness of this age, against spiritual hosts of wickedness in the heavenly places. Therefore take up the whole armor of God, that you may be able to withstand in the evil day, and having done all, to stand. Stand therefore, having girded your waist with truth, having put on the breastplate of righteousness, and having shod your feet with the preparation of the gospel of peace; above all, taking the shield of faith with which you will be able to quench all the fiery darts of the wicked one. And take the helmet of salvation, and the sword of the Spirit, which is the word of God; praying always with all prayer and supplication in the Spirit, being watchful to this end with all perseverance and supplication for all the saints—and for me, that utterance may be given to me, that I may open my mouth boldly to make known the mystery of the gospel, for which I am an ambassador in chains; that in it I may speak boldly, as I ought to speak.
> (Ephesian 6:10-20)

We will see a brave and bold army arise this year as we obey God. We can be strong in the Lord and the power of His might! This is our birthright; our family heritage. We have come to the kingdom for such a time as this. BE BRAVE!

Be strong

Nehemiah taught us where our strength comes from:

> Then he said to them, "Go your way, eat the fat, drink the sweet, and send portions to those for whom nothing is prepared; for this day is holy to our Lord. Do not sorrow, for the joy of the LORD is your strength."
> (Nehemiah 8:10)

The joy of the Lord keeps us strong. Do not let the enemy steal your joy in 2021. We can be a rejoicing people. Thanksgiving, praise, and worship keep us in the place of joy. Thank Him for who He is! Praise Him for His mighty power! Worship Him as King of Kings and Lord of Lords! Be strong in the Lord! God will strengthen you this year. Wait on Him and watch what happens.

> He gives power to the weak,
> And to those who have no might He increases strength.
> Even the youths shall faint and be weary,
> And the young men shall utterly fall,
> But those who wait on the LORD
> Shall renew their strength;
> They shall mount up with wings like eagles,
> They shall run and not be weary,
> They shall walk and not faint. (Isaiah 40:29-31)

God is coming with power and strength in 2021!

Finally, let everything be done in love

We are reminded again to make sure everything is done in love. We are to be a people motivated by love. We can even love our enemies,

"You have heard that it was said, 'You shall love your neighbor and hate your enemy.' But I say to you, love your enemies, bless those who curse you, do good to those who hate you, and pray for those who spitefully use you and persecute you, that you may be sons of your Father in heaven; for He makes His sun rise on the evil and on the good, and sends rain on the just and on the unjust. For if you love those who love you, what reward have you? Do not even the tax collectors do the same? And if you greet your brethren only, what do you do more than others? Do not even the tax collectors do so? Therefore you shall be perfect, just as your Father in heaven is perfect." (Matthew 56:43-48)

> God is bringing us into oneness of heart and encouraging us to love one another like Jesus has loved us. This is how people will know that we are His disciples.

Love and pray your enemies into the kingdom. Love never fails.

Love never fails. But whether there are prophecies, they will fail; whether there are tongues, they will cease; whether there is knowledge, it will vanish away. (1 Corinthians 13:8)

As we are motivated by love we will see God move this year. Keeping ourselves in the love of God will position us to see God's kingdom come and will be done. Remember what love does: it "bears all things, believes all things, hopes all things, endures all things." (1 Corinthians 13:7)

In 2021 we will need to endure, bear with each other, believe and hope; and God's love will conquer! Remember:

Who shall separate us from the love of Christ? Shall tribulation, or distress, or persecution, or famine, or nakedness, or peril, or sword? As it is written: "For Your sake we are killed all day long; We are accounted as sheep for the slaughter." Yet in all these things we are more than conquerors through Him who loved us. For I am persuaded that neither death nor life, nor angels nor principalities nor powers, nor things present nor things to come, nor height nor depth, nor any other created thing, shall be able to separate us from the love of God which is in Christ Jesus our Lord. (Romans 8:35-39)

THE GREATEST IS LOVE. May God draw us to Himself and prepare us for the coming year.

Abbey McCracken

Abbey McCracken is a young prophetic voice who has been hearing God's voice since she was three years old. She grew up in a prophetic household hearing testimonies of what God is doing.

She has ministered in public schools, private schools, ministry schools, churches, conferences, in the marketplace, and in social settings, and her prophetic accuracy at such a young age has amazed leaders and recipients.

In spring 2020, Abbey graduated high school and college, simultaneously. She has been serving as interim Youth Pastor at her local church, but in January 2021 will transition into Youth With A Mission (YWAM).

Abbey's desire is to walk in the fullness of her calling as a prophetic voice in the nations. She is eager to see captives set free and walking in their godly, royal destinies with a new perspective of who they are, and who God is!

7
A VISION OF THE SEVEN MOUNTAINS
Abbey McCracken

So, as I prayed about what God wanted to do and say about 2021, I saw a valley surrounded by seven different, dark-colored mountains. Three of the seven mountains were made of jet-black coal. Another three were covered with dead, rotted trees. And the last mountain was a gigantic pile of ashes. I felt the Lord was showing me the Seven Mountains, as described in Bill Johnson and Lance Wallnau's book *Invading Babylon: The 7 Mountain Mandate*.

The mountains were arranged in a circle with the religion mountain at the top, then going clockwise were government, education, economy, media, arts, and family. I asked the Lord what each mountain was; He said the dark coal mountains were Media, Arts, and Education. The mountains with dead, rotted trees were Government, Economy, and Family. The mountain of ashes was Religion. I focused on the valley formed by these mountains and saw lightning and a downpour of rain. Dense fog circled the upper edges of the valley and brushed the peak of every mountain.

The mountains of religion and government sat next to each other. And between these mountains a group of soldiers marched into the valley. Each soldier looked different—they were different genders and ages, wearing various styles of armor. Some wore clean, untouched and polished silver, while others had on armor that was battered and tarnished. But you could feel the anticipation for what God was going to do in and through each of the soldiers.

What I feel the Lord saying through this vision is that He is building a new army. The church, or mountain of Religion, has been dead too long. The Lord wants to bring His church back to her identity as His beautiful bride. He will bring beauty from ashes—total transformation of the church. The mountains of dark rock that are Education, Media, and Art have been plagued for too long by a darkness that seems to be unshakeable and unbreakable; a lost cause. But the Lord is calling for a shaking and a breaking of these mountains! He will give influence to His people in those mountains, and they will bring kingdom principles that will affect the nations.

The rotting trees on the other three mountains represent fallen and broken leaders. These compromised leaders will be replaced or restored as they are willing to work with the Lord. I see the Lord saying He made these mountains to grow. As they grow they get taller to touch heaven. God wants to partner with the spheres of Government, Family, and Economy to cause them to align with the wisdom of Heaven. He wants to give them a "kingdom stamp," declaring His kingdom over them.

The soldiers are a new breed of Christian. They are the disciples who will go into these mountains and change the culture. In this season beginning with the year 2021, the Lord is not looking for people with titles or public platforms. He is looking for obedient soldiers that will fight for kingdom values. His call has never been about age, race, or gender, and He is not focused on people's past. His mandate involves heaven coming to earth.

The fog over the valley covered the mountain peaks because it covered truth, godly truth. It was meant to keep believers in a fogged state of mind that blocked out heaven's realities, so they could only believe what they presently saw manifested on the various mountains.

In 2020 the Lord was revealing and reforming the church, families, trust in God, governments, and elections that will continue into 2021, but this is the year we are going to have to put feet to our faith to walk out what God has shown us; to accomplish what God is wanting to do through us.

Davids are going to arise in 2021; yes, this means people who haven't had a "perfect" Christian life. But they have a heart for the Lord. The Lord is calling us to dance like David in this season. Dance over defeat, dance over promises, dance until you get the victory. There is such overwhelming grace in this year for people who are undone in the presence of Lord. This will be a clean hands and pure heart movement. Purity is a weapon that is unstoppable. The enemy has tried to strip purity off children, but the Lord is bringing childlike faith and purity to be unstoppable and untouchable. This purity will cause people to have access to His presence in a way we have yet to see. This isn't just a purity of our physical bodies; the Lord is saying that if we are washed by the blood, the blood always washes us white as snow. Stepping into this purity gives us access and strategy like no other generation. We are currently facing crazy things that need Jesus's answers. His answers take down giants. David didn't need a gun or a sword; he needed the King of all kings. When he picked up the five smooth pebbles, victory seemed impossible. But God is the King of the impossible, and He grabs hold of a narrative of defeat and declares victory.

> This will be a clean hands and pure heart movement. Purity is a weapon that is unstoppable.

The Lord is going to reveal the spirit realm. We will see angels and demons in the natural world. There will be less of a veil between these two realms; the spirits on people will be revealed. Churches and Christians will need to be equipped with the knowledge of how to take out these spirits. These spirits are going to fight for ground, but this is a year of taking back the ground. They have made themselves too comfortable in churches, families, government, Hollywood, social media, and our daily lives. But the "despicables" are going to rise up to take back the kingdom. We will see the things the Bible talks about in the New Testament, with demons being revealed and being cast out! They are going to fight tooth and nail, but the power and authority the Lord has given us will be our strength. We are stepping into—and have been stepping into—a new season.

Don't lose hope; the Author has already written the story and we win! We will arise; we will see the impossible made possible!

Bobby Haaby

Bobby is a catalyst and thought leader who encourages and provokes the church to put "Apostolic feet to Prophetic hope." As a Senior Leader of Eagle Mountain, an Apostolic Resource Center in Bend Oregon, Bobby thrives in creating an atmosphere where powerful people can run together and partner with God to release heaven on earth.

Called to serve the Lord through an audible voice encounter, Bobby has given his life to see Christianity defined by the tangible presence of God, through an atmosphere of training, discipleship, and signs and wonders, and by releasing heaven's blueprints for societal transformation to solve the world's most pressing problems. Bobby believes the world is desperate for an encounter with the Living God, and that we are witnessing the emerging of the sons and daughters that all creation has been waiting for.

8

A NEW GOVERNMENT
Bobby Haaby

The Day the Trumpet Fell

On March 21, 2020, I heard the Holy Spirit shouting "3...2...1...LAUNCH!"

In this encounter, I knew that the "launch" had to do with the emerging voices that God is releasing all over the planet; a new breed of apostolic and prophetic trumpets rising that possess the language of the Spirit to clearly articulate and mobilize the strategies of heaven. I was shown that these emerging voices of influence are individuals who have no intention of satisfying the "itching ears" spoken of in 2 Timothy chapter four. They have received a revelation of the Lord's love, they have broken through into victory over spirits of intimidation and the fear of man, and they are ready to shape the future from a position of intimacy and authority.

These emerging voices are "apostolic" because they have received an impartation that comes from being shown the value of mobilizing the people of God. They are "prophetic" because they have learned how to stand at their post and keep watch to see what heaven is saying. They are both apostolic and prophetic because they have learned how to put "apostolic feet to prophetic hope" and mobilize God's end-time army.

Can you imagine if Joseph had only given half of the word of the Lord?

Perhaps he could have released a word like, "There is a famine coming and God has a plan for us to 'arise and shine' and His glory will be seen around the world, and the greatest revival will be sure to follow"?

Can you imagine if heaven forgot to give Joseph the strategy Pharoah needed to store up supplies for seven years? Even though Egypt was an ungodly nation, if the leaders would listen to heaven's strategy and diligently walk it out, their nation would come through the famine with plenty, enough to be generous to surrounding nations; and specifically God's people. Can you imagine if Joseph left out the strategic side of the prophetic? What if he didn't know how to interpret heaven's dreams and only gave the encounter, but not the strategy? As "end-time" scenarios unfold, the demand on the apostolic and prophetic communities will increase. We must learn to go beyond initial encounters and revelatory information and look closely for strategies from heaven. This is a timely mandate that requires both the apostolic and the prophetic anointing to collaborate. It is the cloak of "many colors."

There is a BIG difference between prophetic foresight and commentary. The first happens before the incident occurs and the other after the incident is assessed. Surely, we can glean wisdom once an event has unfolded, but that is different from receiving prophetic foresight. When it came to mobilizing God's people, it was rare for a prophet in the Bible to give a word without the strategy to carry it out. Is it possible that we, as a prophetic community, have become accustomed to running to our platforms with the initial encounter but don't turn aside to inquire of the Lord for strategy on how to walk it out? In the Bible, the "Sons of Issachar" knew the times and seasons AND how to mobilize Israel. Shouldn't this be the measure that helps us to build on the foundation of the apostles and prophets? Now, we will go deeper in our prophetic revelation, begin to humbly collaborate with and even seek out, people who challenge us, and we will find that this is key to walking out the "apostolic feet to prophetic hope" mandate.

Little did I know, when I received this download from heaven, that three days prior, on March 18, 2020, Salt Lake City had just experienced an earthquake with a magnitude of 5.7. The Mormon Tabernacle, built in 1893, was severely shaken. On the top tower there is a statue of an angel named "Moroni," who Mormons claim is an ancient prophet that led founder Joseph Smith to the golden plate from which the book of Mormon was translated. The image stands at the pinnacle of their tabernacle holding a trumpet to his mouth. When the earthquake hit, Moroni's trumpet was broken off and fell to the ground.

God spoke to me and said that will be a day in history: "The Day the Trumpet Fell." He said that there would arise apostolic and prophetic voices that were appointed directly from heaven to bring heaven's culture to earth and shape society, not just by what they will say, but by what they will do. Abraham, who is called a "prophet" and "the father of our faith" never spoke a message recorded in the Bible. There is nothing wrong with having and being a voice. But God wanted the "father of our faith" known, not for what he said, but for what he did. These emerging voices will be true fathers and mothers of faith who have learned the truth of 1 Corinthians 4:20:

> The kingdom of God is not a matter of words, but of power.

Leading the Global RESET

Noah built an ARK during the time of a flood. It was the first global reset.

The ark was bigger than he imagined, took longer to build than he imagined, and the building process began many years before it was needed.

As the globe grew darker spiritually, there was Noah building, possibly feeling that he was way outside of his season. No one around him could see the vision. He was building for the future. It had never rained before.

Have you ever felt like you were building for another season?

The church has a mandate to innovate and build the kingdom in every sphere of society. I know that there is a bit of insecurity in building something that has never been built before, but if we wait for the trends and the markets to confirm our vision, we will already be behind the curve, waiting for external circumstances to confirm our heavenly vision.

> **Emerging voices have learned how to put "apostolic feet to prophetic hope" and mobilize God's end-time army.**

In the kingdom, it is too late to start building a boat after rain begins. The blueprints from heaven are often given long before there is even a cloud in the atmosphere. We are learning to lead a global rest, and that requires us to overcome the insecurity of not having a fully completed set of blueprints. Heaven's blueprints unfold and appear in greater detail as we individually make the decision that it is safer with Jesus on the raging sea than in the boat without Him.

Characteristics of the Ark

The ark did not have a rudder. How could Noah spend 120 years building this massive vision and forget to attach the most important device that would drive and navigate the vision through high waters to its destination? This tells me a few things.

1. God is confident in His navigating skills and is so prophetic that He begins with your end-game in mind.
2. Woven within His bestowed favor is the grace to be led by the dove. In other words, "You're not big enough to screw this up." The Holy Spirit is a master at getting us onboard with heaven's purpose for our lives.

3. The door could only be closed from the outside, which means that, in this season, God will determine who gets into your boat.
4. The boat required rain; something supernatural from heaven for it to launch. What you are building is so supernatural that it requires heaven to pour down something that has yet to be released.
5. The dove had to be sent out many times to determine if the vision was landing in the right place at the right time. Christianity is often the one group in society that does not possess a research and development department. God is bringing a shift in our perception of how "heaven on earth" is established as we learn to interact with the dove—the Holy Spirit.

Innovation requires that we make a ton of mistakes. Our mindset shift must occur in the way we filter our "mistakes." Are they seen as failures or discoveries? Allowing others to make mistakes is a huge part of an R&D atmosphere. We all love to be around people like us, but God is building relationships and teams around diversity. It's so easy to operate from an "I love the me that I see in you" mentality; we like to define this as "community" or "I found my tribe." Sameness will never create unity because unity can never be found in conformity, sentimental connection, or in similar gifting. This is why individuals with the "Five-fold Ministry" gifts found in Ephesians chapter four were given different lenses through which they could see the kingdom. This was never meant to dilute the truth, but was a foundation for requiring collaboration to discover "all truth."

As long as we remain suspicious of those who don't see things that way we do, the true "bond of the Spirit" will elude us. God is not only bringing people to us who have a different perspective, but He is asking us to be brave enough to seek them out. Our relationships and teams should be filled with people who are not like us. God is placing

His mouth to trumpets—voices who are not satisfied with being an "echo" of their favorite five people. He is releasing His breath through those who are willing to be a "voice" from heaven. Finding your voice is about entering into a partnership that is birthed out of intimate conversation with God. God wants you to value what He has created in you enough for you to join the conversation. Your Creator has given you a life story, and that journey has given you a unique thumb print and a voice that no one else has.

Religion has always sought to silence the voice of God and the voice of His bride. You have something to say because you are seated with Him. Religion would prefer that we remain an echo while your chair next to the throne is left unoccupied. Begin by valuing yourself enough to hear what is inside your heart. God says "You are about to discover who you really are." The Scriptures say that God's voice is as the sound of many waters (see Ezekiel 43:2). But in the book of Revelation, at the end of the age, only one other voice is described as having the very same sound: the church. (see Rev 19:6). Our voice is as the sound of many waters, just like His.

The Most Prepared People On The Planet
Hebrews 11:7 reveals a profound key for leading the global reset.

> By Faith Noah being warned about things unseen, in reverence, built an ARK...

I want to extract five words from this verse that I feel the Holy Spirit is highlighting in this hour.
- Faith.
- Warned.
- Unseen.
- Reverence.
- Built.

Faith

There is a difference between having "faith in God" and possessing the "faith of God." God is releasing new realities of the "Christ in you, the hope of glory" and the world is beginning to see what God meant when the apostle Paul said "It is no longer I who lives, but Christ who lives in me..." (see Galatians 2:20). We are receiving an upgrade in the reality of Jesus living His life through us by the Holy Spirit. The very God who was reconciling the world to Himself through His Son Jesus, while He walked the earth, has by His genius plan, become the God in Christ in you.

Warned

God wants to share His insights and intel with us before things happen. He is giving us the invitation to look higher than the plans of the enemy found in second heaven revelation. Heaven's strategies are found above the level of discerning what the enemy plans to do. Heaven's strategies unfold as we position ourselves to receive solutions to the world's pressing problems. This begins by asking God for strategies for our friends, our regions, our churches, and the places God has given us influence. Discoveries in many spheres of society will be revealed in the coming few years. We will see heaven unlock discoveries in medicine, government, technology, space, just to name a few. The "Rude Awakening" of the COVID-19 controversy is being used by God to allow the required tension to create the "Great Awakening" that the church has been believing for.

> The "Sons of Issachar" knew the times and seasons AND how to mobilize Israel. Shouldn't this be the measure that helps us to build on the foundation of the apostles and prophets?

Unseen

The year 2020 was a pivotal point in helping us to see just how much we do not see. We have felt the tension and fear of those who look to the seen realm more than the unseen realm. We have also seen our need for the Holy Spirit to touch our eyes with heavenly eye salve so we can view reality the way heaven sees it. We will shine with revelation for those around us who need the supernatural ability to see what already exists in the unseen realm. It will be like sharing your EnChroma® Spirit glasses with those who cannot see in living color and watching their reality come to life.

Reverence

We must reverence the word of the Lord enough to prepare for its fulfillment. This was the engine behind Noah's ark; his reverence for the word of God. As prophetic people, we are called to be the most prepared people on the planet. We are to be the most innovative, and we are to feel right at home in the mystery of God. Many think that the prophetic gift is synonymous with being spontaneous and unplanned. But the very gift, by nature, found in the "Spirit of Elijah" was created to prepare the way of the Lord. If we are going to lead a global reset, we have to revere the reality that it was God who told us to build. Then we must take our words off the shelf and ask the Holy Spirit how to prepare and begin to build.

Built

You might have said, or heard it said, "If God wants my vision to happen, He'll make it happen," which may sound like faith and trust. The only problem with that statement is that it requires no ownership. This season is about God partnering with you and you allowing your vision to reach the recesses of your heart's desire, to the point where you are energized by the Holy Spirit to a level of commitment to be faithful to build the heavenly vision. If our vision just stays in the revelatory realm and does not touch desire, then we will have difficulty being "all in" and showing up 100 percent for a revelation that has only reached our vision realm. This is a season to allow our heart to be healed from the disillusionment of unfulfilled desires. We must re-engage our desire and allow it to be cleansed by the Lord so that the seeds of revelation can germinate. This is the season where our spirits, souls, and bodies will be congruent and in alignment with God. It's one thing to walk in John 17 unity with our brother, but true unity requires that we first get in unity with our triune selves and fully believe in our destiny, building from a position of being fully persuaded.

Your Favor Factor
We are not living *for* favor; we are living *FROM* favor.

This is a perspective shift that heaven is releasing to God's people. This perspective will shift how we pray and how we shape the planet with our decrees. If our prayer life, intercession, and prophetic anointing primarily function from an "earth to heaven" reality, then we will be limited to a prayer life of "asking and contending." There is nothing wrong with asking God to do great things and prophesying that He will. The shift that the Holy Spirit is bringing to our prayer life in this hour will enable us to use the intimacy of our relationship with God to shape the landscape of society from our positions of authority. It is there that we move beyond operating from an "earth to heaven" asking reality and begin operating from a "heaven to earth" decreeing reality.

In a recent encounter in the Holy of Holies I was shown that for many in the body of Christ, (me included), the apex of our life in Christ has been to experience face-to-face encounters of friendship and intimacy with Him. In this encounter I was beyond the veil, kneeling in front of God with an ardent desire to see Him again. He sternly said "Stand up and take your place next to Me." He continued, "Your intimacy has granted you authority to take this scepter."

I was on my knees facing Him when he said this, and instinctively I knew that I needed to get up quickly and take my place next to Him. As I transitioned from facing Him to standing next to Him, I was hit with the reality that together He and I were facing out from the Holy of Holies and had heaven's view of the entire planet. He interrupted my thoughts and said, "What will you decree from this place to a planet that desperately needs you to shape its future by what comes out of your mouth"?

Suddenly my whole perspective changed to a new reality that intimacy and friendship with God were never designed to enable us to be narcissistic. It is possible to get used to enjoying wonder-filled experiences with God without being aware that He wants to transform our understanding of how to love and teach us what we get to do with our royalty. I realized that I had been spending my favor on myself mostly, and not shaping the landscape of the planet that we were given.

> **We are not living FOR favor, we are living FROM favor.**

So, I began learning to use my favor, intimacy, and authority well. I began to move beyond soulish sentiment and learned to partner with heaven to create the future for my wife, family, friends, church, region, nations, and for my globe. I took ownership of the reality that Psalm 115:16 reveals:

> The heavens are the heavens of the Lord,
> But the earth He has given to the sons of mankind.
> (NASB)

> The heavens belong to our God; they are his alone,
> but he has given us the earth and put us in charge.
> (TPT)

The intimacy with Christ and the time spent in His Word that you and God cultivate through the years creates the pure motivation required to hold the scepter and make decrees that shape the future. This is equivalent to the moment in Genesis when God was creating the heavens and the earth and every living thing. When finished, He called Adam to His side to let Adam name the animals. God could have done that alone, but He refused to finish creating without allowing Adam—whose name means man—to create with Him.

The invitation to create with Him from a place of intimacy and authority still exists. He has not finished creating and we are still invited to help. To wield the sword of the Spirit, we must first have been cut by it. We are called to possess a willingness to allow the Spirit of God to use His Word to call us beyond operating primarily from our souls to operating out of our spirits, which work in relationship with His Spirit. This is why you have been in a pressure cooker of sorts. He has been training you to use your favor well.

Laws of Attraction

In this season, as your life and destiny in God unfolds, the Holy Spirit is bringing you into a divine convergence to position you for a continual increase in wisdom, stature, and favor. The Spirit of God in you will attract people to you who are designed to serve God's purposes that you carry.

> And Jesus kept increasing in wisdom and stature, and in favor with God and men. (Luke 2:52, NASB)

"Wisdom" is the application of your knowledge and the supernatural ability to turn your encounters and dreams with God into reality. This increase in the Spirit of wisdom is being poured out to give you the capacity to clearly recognize where your favor should be directed right now. In the Bible the "Sons of Issachar" knew the times (Greek kairos: the NOW opportunities) and the seasons. Not all open doors should be walked through. This wisdom is created to serve the favor you walk in, so that you keep in step with God in every season.

"Stature" refers to the size of your heart and your inner man. It's a combination of your God-sized dreams, His presence in your life, and the size of your YES to God. Your stature in the Spirit will cause people to recognize Gods purpose and presence in your life and will be used by Him to attract favor with men.

Favor is a direct result of grace and is the engine for your vision. Favor causes whatever you need, and even desire, to be made manifest.

> And God is able to make all grace (favor) abound to you, so that always having all sufficiency in everything, you may have an abundance for every good deed.
> (2 Corinthians 9:8, NASB)

Favor is so powerful that it requires wisdom to steward properly. Favor without wisdom results in lack of readiness when your moment arrives. But favor with wisdom increases your stature, the ability to be recognized, and causes you to live in a constant state of flow and congruence with God and men. He has designed us to straddle two realms at the same time. We stand before people and yet operate from a heavenly reality. Congruence happens when both heaven and earth are seamlessly functioning without tension in our lives and we are living the life that God designed us to live. Growing in receiving and giving favor is a huge part of kingdom life.

Remember: Favor without the anointing and presence of God on your life is like having a Ferrari without any fuel; how would you be able to operate it?

Spending Your Favor

The secret to your increase in these NOW moments is directly linked to recognizing and valuing your "burning bush" (new and uncommon) invitations and your ability to "take off your shoes" and stay a while with Him. God set a precedent for Moses and taught him to not take lightly His strange ways of getting Moses' attention and drawing him into a continual flow of supernatural thought-traffic. Moses not only turned aside to encounter God's obvious and explosive invitations, but he also built a dwelling place for continual encounters and called it the "Tent of Meeting." From that day on, everyone knew Moses was intentional about using his favor to get more favor.

In Exodus 33:13, Moses discovers how to use his favor.

> "Now therefore, I pray You, if I have found favor in Your sight, let me know Your ways that I may know You, so that I may find favor in Your sight."

Did you catch it? Moses uses his favor with God to get closer to God, and know His ways, so he may find more favor with God. This bold *ask* launches Moses into a staggering discovery that God's presence in his life is the ultimate measurement for all true favor. In a production-minded culture, God is reminding us that He wants us to first use our favor to encounter Him. Then, from a place of favor, authority, and power, we will partner with Him to serve and save this world, operating from a deep well that will never run dry.

Favor and Friendship

Exodus 33:14-16 reads:

> And He said, "My presence shall go with you, and I will give you rest." Then he said to Him, "If Your presence does not go with us, do not lead us up from here. For how then can it be known that I have found favor in Your sight, I and Your people? Is it not by Your going with us, so that we, I and Your people, may be distinguished from all the other people who are upon the face of the earth?"

Moses had learned from his surprise "burning bush" encounters, and from wearing a path in the sand to his regularly scheduled "Tent of Meeting" moments with God, that experiencing more of God's presence would cause him to go from favor to friendship.

Moses grew in favor and confidence in God because his ultimate assignment was to walk in such an experiential reality of favor and friendship with God that it would attract the tangible glory of God to this planet.

Then Moses said, "I pray You, show me Your glory!"

Have you ever admired someone's favor? You have found the favor and the friendship of God who is saying the very same words to you that Joshua heard from the Lord after watching Moses's life.

"I will be with you just as I was with Moses." (Joshua 1:5)

God is increasing the reality of His presence in your life. He loves you and He likes you. He doesn't just tolerate you because of His love. He genuinely likes being with you.

Apostolic Administrators

So, you might be asking "how do I sense what God is saying, prepare for greatness, and build an ark without a rudder; how do I get a vision that can't be controlled by me?

There is a difference between control and stewardship.

We need the innovators, futurists, revelators, and creatives to shape society through their vision and narrative. But we also need strategists; people with Holy Spirit-led administrative gifts who can take a vision and create blueprints for our lives, businesses, and ministries. This apostolic administration has been overlooked in many "revival cultures," but this is actually a huge part of the foundation of the apostolic gift. We will seek apostolic administrators that will challenge us to move beyond revelation into mobilization. We will revere and welcome them; they are about to be valued as a great gift from heaven and will find their place among the apostolic and prophetic communities.

The world is beginning to experience an *ekklesia* type church that knows how to solve the planet's most pressing problems. This requires us to operate from the mindset that we are not just hoping that God will fund our dream, but we actually have a mandate from heaven, given directly from God to steward. We will operate from the reality that we have unlimited resources at our disposal.

The eight people that entered the ark did so with the mindset that they needed to be saved from a global RESET, but the eight people who exited that ark had been transformed and were now operating from the mindset that they were anointed to start a brand new civilization and release things on the planet that had never been seen before.

Question: We have to ask ourselves, What if the Scriptures that state "as in the days of Noah, so shall it be in the coming of the son of man" do not just refer to an overwhelming end-time scenario full of darkness that we are escaping from? But what if it also refers to a powerful remnant of people who, like Noah, have a mandate to release God's *new* and God's *next* on the planet?

God is releasing the Noahs who are anointed to create new civilizations of thought, revelation, technology, science, and apostolic environments that this planet has yet to experience.

Raising the Watermark

Blueprints include calculations for structural integrity, and they also map out elevations. Elevations speak of our perspective and the ability to imagine on Gods level. The elevation indicators on your heavenly blueprints also speak of maturity and give us a picture of the type of people God is raising up right now.

This is why God has been strengthening your inner man.

The Spirit of God has been taking us from IQ (intellectual quotient) to building our EQ (emotional quotient) so that we can carry a healthy SQ (spiritual quotient). We are moving from prioritizing, valuing, and operating out of the concepts that our minds can comprehend (IQ) into valuing and prioritizing how we show up emotionally in our relationships and how we make space for the powerful people that God has placed around us. As we learn to create this part of the culture of heaven, not only will it release supernatural levels of honor and maturity, but it will release our Spiritual Quotient (SQ) to soar and operate at high levels.

A House of Powerful People

In a recent encounter I was approaching an old house. I was taken directly to a bedroom window opening where I could see and hear two brothers talking. They were lying down as if they had just awakened from sleep. I knew instinctively that the two brothers were James and Jesus. I watched as Jesus told James of the dream he had that night and how the Father spoke to him. I quickly looked at James's face to see how he was processing the amazing encounter that Jesus was explaining. I instantly could hear James's thoughts and the struggle that he was having with Jesus's frequent encounters with the Father. I could hear James thinking, "He always gets encounters like this; how come I don't?"

I quickly looked back at Jesus to see if He could sense this. Would Jesus stop to appease James? But Jesus never dumbed-down His brilliance to make James feel better. He did notice the jealousy and insecurity that was rising in his brother James, but He finished telling His story, giving James the opportunity to stay engaged and celebrate Jesus. The second that Jesus finished explaining the encounter, He quickly said, "James, you hear from the Father in different ways than I do. Tell me what He has been speaking to you?" I watched Jesus pull treasures out of His brother by asking the right questions. It was like watching Jesus draw water out of a deep well. Jesus was creating space for his brother to come alive and James was now fully engaged.

That is when the Lord interrupted the encounter and said, "This is how it should be in My house."

Imagine what it was like to grow up in a household with Jesus.

The church was designed to operate the same way. Jesus' mom was Mary, who will forever be known as the woman who gave birth to the Savior of the world. Jesus' step-dad, Joseph, was from the royal line of David, His uncle Zechariah was a priest from the line of Aaron, and His cousin was John the Baptist who was called "More than a prophet... and among those born of a woman, there is no one greater."

And then there was Jesus, who had a star show up at His birth. Are you getting the picture of where God is taking the church? Jesus knows what it is like to grow up in a house of powerful people. We must now learn how to not dumb down our brilliance, while intentionally creating space for those around us; especially for those who may be struggling with your amazingness.

Did you know that Jesus had siblings? Yes, He had to learn to allow Himself to "happen" while creating space and opportunity for His brothers and sisters to "happen."

> He came to His hometown and began teaching them in their synagogue, so that they were astonished, and said, "Where did this man get this wisdom and these miraculous powers? Is not this the carpenter's son? Is not His mother called Mary, and His brothers, James and Joseph and Simon and Judas? And His sisters, are they not all with us? Where then did this man get all these things?" And they took offense at Him. But Jesus said to them, "A prophet is not without honor except in his hometown and in his own household." And He did not do many miracles there because of their unbelief.
> (Matthew 13:54-58)

The words used here for "brothers" and "sisters" are in the literal tense. Although they were not conceived by the Holy Spirit like Jesus, these were not spiritual siblings but actual siblings who had to learn to grow up together and would have available to them the same indwelling Holy Spirit Jesus had. It is also stated that Jesus's brothers may not have believed that He was the Messiah until after the resurrection. According to the apostle John, "not even his brothers (literal) believed in him" (John 7:5).

That's incredible. Those who had lived with Jesus for over thirty years really did not know Him entirely. Is that even possible? Can you really get that close to God, or something He is doing in the earth, and still not believe? Not one of Jesus's 'brothers is mentioned as a disciple during His pre-crucifixion ministry. But after his resurrection and ascension, they were found in the upper room worshiping Him as God (Acts 1:14).

It is not surprising that God used James to be the foremost authority in the Bible on subjects like faith, jealousy, partiality, unbelief and double-mindedness. James didn't just sit down one day to write a book, he lived it. He knew what it was like to overcome huge amounts of insecure thought traffic and the struggle to find his identity in Christ, his brother. It is moving to hear James later refer to his brother as "our Lord Jesus Christ, the Lord of glory" (James 2:1). Can you imagine what this phrase meant for James? The Lord of glory had once slept beside him, ate at the same dinner table, played with his friends, and dreamt with him about changing the world.

You are called into the most powerful family on the planet—the church. You are about to see your brothers and sisters release things upon the earth that eye has not seen, or ear has not heard before, such as innovation and breakthroughs in technology, signs and wonders and miracles, unprecedented kingdom wealth for the end-time global harvest, and societal transformation. If we can hear Him, Jesus is teaching us how to be powerful un-apologetically. He is also teaching us how to create space for our brothers and sisters to also be powerful un-apologetically. And James is teaching us how to overcome the tendency to compare ourselves to other powerful people or get jealous when they walk in something we long to accomplish. In a household of powerful people, we really are a team and we succeed when our brother succeeds. James teaches us how to make space for powerful, anointed people while learning to allow ourselves to "happen" at the same time.

Marketing yourself or your company does not need to consist of slogans that highlight the deficiency of others. It's good to have a healthy drive and even be competitive. But the best way to separate yourself and achieve the lion's share of your market is by doing what you do well, not by stating to the public what others don't do.

The true definition of "powerful people" is not just found in a group of high-level executives in three-piece suits. It can be;but "powerful people" are mostly defined by knowing who they are and whose they are. The have learned to serve and rule with the heart of royalty. They have learned that they need each other and have found a way to create space for each other to happen and transform the world around them.

Two Anointings: Presence and Power

I see two anointings increasing on the church right now that will launch us into a balanced kingdom life of "faith" and "works."

The Bible says in 1 John 2:27

> As for you, the anointing which you received from Him abides in you, and you have no need for anyone to teach you; but as His anointing teaches you about all things, and is true and is not a lie, and just as it has taught you, you abide in Him.

This anointing is given to reveal GOD TO US. Acts 1: 8 tells us

> "...but you will receive power when the Holy Spirit has come upon you; and you shall be My witnesses both in Jerusalem, and in all Judea and Samaria, and even to the remotest part of the earth."

This anointing is also given to reveal GOD THROUGH US.

It is a tragedy watching someone try to feed themselves from the spiritual high of the Acts 1:8 "power anointing." This anointing can never take the place of our 1 John 2 "presence anointing," because one anointing was given to know Him and the other was given to make Him known. Knowing God is our first priority, and as our faith increases we will long to see His kingdom manifest. We are called to live from His presence and release His power and purpose on the earth. YOU CAN HAVE BOTH ANOINTINGS.

Read James 2:18-20 where he tells us,

> But someone may well say, "You have faith and I have works; show me your faith without the works, and I will show you my faith by my works." You believe that God is one. You do well; the demons also believe, and shudder. But are you willing to recognize, you foolish fellow, that faith without works is useless?"

Find your tribe and love them well

In an atmosphere and culture of faith, you will find that a trait of powerful people is the reality of this Scripture; the awareness that "faith without works is useless." Faith-filled people want to see God and they want to see results. To allow powerful people to "happen" around you, or to create space for them, means that we commit to not put down their need to produce, work, or perform.

The desire to see results does not automatically mean that these mobilizers are living in a state of "doing" instead of "being." I have seen insecure people judge powerful people too quickly in this way. Do we all still need to balance rest, relationship, and works? YES. But, the way community works well in an apostolic tribe of powerful people is that we are called to get close enough to each other to recognize that when one is in need of "presence," we create space for them by taking a few tasks off their shoulders and helping them to achieve their desire for more of God's presence. This works to help "presence" driven people find balance in community and dial up "purpose" when needed. Likewise, if someone needs "purpose" we help them understand and create a strategy to carry His presence into community and walk in their Acts 1:8 anointing, fulfilling their purpose. God is increasing divine strategy for loving Him and for carrying His love to the world in divine partnership. Abraham, who is called the "father of faith" never stood before a large crowd of people and gave a great eloquent message to mobilize the masses like many other leaders in the Bible. He was known as the "father of faith" not by what he said, but by what he did.

James 2:21-23 states

> Was not Abraham our father justified by works when he offered up Isaac his son on the altar? You see faith was working with his works, and as a result of the works, faith was perfected; and the Scripture was fulfilled which says, "And Abraham believed God, and it was reckoned to him as righteousness," and he was called the friend of God.

You are part of a great new era of kings and priests who are not satisfied until we know God and make Him known. It is time for the Kingdom of God to manifest like we have never seen before, and you have come to the Kingdom for such a time as this. I bless your faith and the work of your hands to multiply.

God is so excited about placing you in a house of powerful people. He is taking His household from slavery to sonship by releasing fathers and mothers. Slaves believe that they have no resources, but fathers allow sons to emerge by showing them that they have unlimited resources. In this season you will have the confidence of Jesus and walk in the abundance of unlimited resources. You will also have the confidence that is produced through humility; the same humility that James learned to possess as you celebrate others and create space for them, while allowing yourself to explode with favor and freedom. The definition that was first given to the house of God is found in Genesis 28:17. It set the bar that the house of God was meant to be known for having access to the supernatural resources of heaven continually.

> "This is none other than the house of God and the portal of Heaven."

The watermark of Christianity is rising. Sons and daughters are not just praying for favor, but rather decreeing from favor. We have understood that we are not waiting for God to change the world, but that He is releasing World Changers who know that they have been sent by God to a planet that belongs to Him. The church is recognizing that a gospel without power is not the gospel of Jesus. True apostles are not satisfied until regions and nations are transformed from within, and the prophetic community is no longer satisfied with giving prophetic commentary after an event has happened and not foretelling it.

The watermark of Christianity is rising! We are no longer seduced by the spirit of accusation, but we are creating the future by what comes out of our mouth. We are becoming consumed with knowing the One who knows all things, and we fully believe that our life in Him is life to others! We are taking nothing for granted as the Church realizes that our steps, our prayers, our strategies, our relationships, and our actions are really ordered of the Lord. We are WELL ABLE to take this land. Do not get caught watching others do exploits while you stand by idly. You have been called for such a time as this!

The Revolution

Modern day Daniels, Josephs, and Esthers are being released who have built credibility through serving their regions and nations of the world. Now, when it counts, they are voices for transformation because they have been at the table serving their regions without agendas. You cannot take to the nations what you have not first pulled off locally. It's there that you gain authority in the Spirit to take to the nations what you have built. God is giving tangible strategy to believers who are willing to roll up their sleeve to serve and love their regions well. There are many ways to serve your region. Whether you are a stay-at-home mom, a business owner, a student, an employee, a child, or retired. Ask the Lord to clarify what sphere of influence He has given you. Start by praying often for that sphere and then look for ways to serve within that arena. God will open up doors for you. But remember, building credibility through consistency is key to growing in your authority in any region.

One major revelation that accompanied the apostolic revolution and the launch of the church was how connected they were to the "great cloud of witnesses." There is a world-wide deliverance that is taking place, right now, in the Body of Christ. It is a deliverance from the "orphan spirit." Being unaware that you are a huge part in a bigger story is the foundation for a life of fear, greed, and socialism. God is releasing the reality that we are standing on the foundation of those who have paved the way for our success. We have been given fathers and mothers, both current and past, whose discoveries are a highway in the Spirit that gives us permission to operate with a green light.

A Supernatural Environment

One of the great things about fathers and mothers who are emerging is that they recognize that leading people into union with Christ means they are introducing people to a supernatural Father who is willing and excited to be the God of breakthrough for us.

When we cut off a supernatural environment from the church as a way of cultivating church, or even home life, there is then no way to get what God can only give. Hope for breakthrough is diminished. This creates a seed bed for an "orphan spirit" because people conclude that they are on their own, and that they have to "survive" their environment. They learn to carry an orphan spirit and a sense of abandonment, and determine that they cannot get what they need from the surrounding environment.

This kind of "orphan" environment focuses mostly on teaching people to suffer well and endure to the end. It is not a supernatural environment where people are introduced to the Father who can supply every need according to His riches in glory. It's an environment where there is no supernatural invasion and therefore, individuals must manipulate to get their needs met. Orphans are consumers; they have relationships or come to church so they can get something.

Why is the revelation that we are LOVED such shocking news to the church? Why is it weird to many that we can crawl up into our Daddy's lap? Many in the church are orphans who are learning to become sons and daughters.

Fathers and mothers supply. They release identity, champion dreams, and provide protection and safety. They release faith for supernatural provision and inheritance, and they cultivate an atmosphere where the reality of God's love positions their spiritual and natural children to operate from a "YES and AMEN" response when they consider allowing themselves to dream.

The Spirit of Adoption

The spirit of adoption introduces into society the idea that there are fathers and mothers who give their lives to establish heaven on earth.

Fathers and mothers are shifting their paradigm and teaching their sons and daughters to grow up to be apostolic in nature, which means that the Church lives from the awareness that we are not human beings having a spiritual experience on earth, but the we are first spirit beings having a human experience.

True fathers and mothers release the reality of a supernatural Father who is bringing heaven to earth and that He answers when we call on His name. We are not afraid to dream, we are not afraid to ask, we are not afraid to give extravagantly, and we are not afraid to trust. God is raising sons and daughter who recognize that the best way to usher in the "new" is to first honor the old. David was allowed by God to build a tabernacle unlike any other. His idea was audacious and had never happened before. David wanted all men to experience the tangible glory of God in a temple with no veil. God granted David his desire with one stipulation. For David to release something on the planet that had never happened before, he had to first go sacrifice where Moses' tabernacle used to be. He had to honor the old before he could release the new. We are often addicted to change and sometimes believe that God is too. But something doesn't have to be wrong in order for God to change it. Jesus said many times "you have heard it said, but now I say to you...". That did not mean that older truths were out of date and irrelevant. It does mean that, in the kingdom, we go from glory to glory and are always increasing because we are connected to a Father who knows no lack.

We are about to received unprecedented revelation about new things that heaven is releasing on the planet. We will do well to not filter heaven's new ideas through an "orphan spirit" and cave to the temptation to dishonor the old to make way for the new. We must have a multi-generational mindset. God is not bringing change into your life because you were doing something wrong. He is multiplying the glory that has been on your life from the beginning. He desires that your bloodline would fulfill the entire testimony which was intended to give Jesus the glory that is due His name. In one life he is able to catch up for many generations.

Futurists become orphans if they don't carry an obligation to history and to those who have gone before them

Sons and orphans see obstacles through entirely different lenses.

What if the obstacles that you are called to overcome are directly linked to the anointing for your assignment? What I'm talking about is higher than the enemy's attacks. This is the realm where you are led by the Spirit to capture an anointing that others will benefit from. Don't waste your seasons!

Breaking Socialism

I recently had an encounter where I saw the false goddess Diana, also called Artemis, raising up out of the ocean posing as the "many breasted one"; the "nurturer of the nations." Her statue shows her as having multiple breasts across her chest. She was beckoning the nations, saying "come to me…" I knew that she was the spirit of socialism and entitlement raising herself up as an imposter and a counterfeit of the great El Shaddai,. one of the Hebrew names for God which means "The Many Breasted One." I saw the Lord break in, smash her to pieces, and judge her. He made a ruling in the courts of heaven which would cause this spirit of socialism and entitlement to have to pay punitive damages.

God is exposing the spirit of socialism and entitlement so that it can be easily identified, and He will cause this spirit to give back what it is attempting to steal. El Shaddai is the God of multiplication. He alone is our source. He is the "Desire of the Nations" (see Haggai 2). We are about to have a Genesis 17 encounter with El Shaddai.

> When Abram was ninety-nine years old, the Lord appeared to him and said, "I am God Almighty [El Shaddai]; walk before me faithfully and be blameless. Then I will make my covenant between me and you and will greatly increase your numbers." Abram fell facedown, and God said to him, "As for me, this is my covenant with you: You will be the father of many nations. No longer will you be called Abram; your name will be Abraham, for I have made you a father of many nations. I will make you very fruitful; I will make nations of you, and kings will come from you…
> (Genesis 17:1-6)

In this encounter, God was releasing upon Abraham the very nature He was coming to Abraham with. This is the level of covenant that God is re-inviting the nations to. God is re-introducing Himself to us, in biblical proportion, as El Shaddai. Because we have chosen to do God's will God's way, He will greatly increase us. He will give us the supernatural ability to multiply and to father and mother nations. I decree to the church: "You are fruitful and a generation of Christians shall now arise who will encounter the reality of the great El Shaddai and who will walk in kingly anointing, governing the earth under this El Shaddai blessing."

In the Bible there were four men of God that served in crisis and captivity. Isaiah prophesied for years about the coming captivity, Jeremiah echoed the word and added the "seventy years" time line, as well as clarifying God's will for Israel to come out of captivity into the plans of God and His hope for their future. Ezekiel prophesied from inside captivity and Daniel prophesied the end of Israel's seventy years of captivity. These men thrived without compromising in crisis because they had solutions from heaven.

Who is praying? Who is hearing from heaven and offering solutions? We are not surprised or confused that a worldly system is worldly. We know that the world is in desperate need of the secrets of heaven that we have access to. It is certainly OK to point out society's problems or to defend the Constitution, but if pointing out the problem is your solution then hear the Lord call you higher. We need solutions! We must get involved and gain credibility in our regions through serving instead of demanding to be heard and demanding to have a seat at a table that we have avoided. Transformation comes through people who find ways to serve their regions and their nations. They gain credibility by doing so without agendas, and then, at the kairos moments, they release a supernatural solution that solves a pressing problem.

To my friends who have contemplated "civil disobedience" as your first response to the overreaches of this pandemic; I understand your frustration. There are lines that will eventually have to be drawn as to how we exercise religious freedom. But first, we must see ourselves as the Daniels, the Esthers, and Josephs that God is raising up and calling to break in to the chaos of the world with solutions from heaven. Our first response as ambassadors of a heavenly kingdom should be "I have access to unlimited resources. How can I help?"

This spirit of royalty that God is releasing on the globe is much more than a "social gospel." It carries high levels of generosity and breaks the fear that exist in socialism and entitlement. We shout to the nations of the world that God is a good Father who is breaking in with all of heaven at His disposal.

> You are called into the most powerful family on the planet. You are about to see your brothers and sisters release things upon the earth that eye has not seen, or ear has not heard before. Jesus is teaching us how to be powerful unapologetically.

We are presently engaged in an economic war with China, who embodies the spirit of socialism. There is a battle raging for who will control the world's economy. Will it be the spirit of socialism and entitlement or will the banner of freedom and free enterprise yet wave? Many in the United States have forfeited true capitalism because they chose to outsource with wrong motives of greed. Greed stifles capitalism because it is the foundation of socialism and entitlement. When someone else is responsible for my freedom and success, or the lack thereof, then I am not free. Now is the time that we can leverage the change that is occurring globally in technology, new discoveries of natural resources, and in world events like COVID-19 and use it to "capitalize" on new ideas that shape our future, or we can continue to mourn what was. The world needs an encounter with those who have been given grace by God to innovate. This is the hour to be overt and no longer covert and let the world around you see Jesus in your brilliant ideas and actions.

What if there is always a shaking before the awakening? What if a rude awakening comes before the Great Awakening? What if the corruption and darkness that is self-evident and is now being revealed is actually being allowed so that you and I will have enough courage to come out of bondage to a system that we have become too dependent on? Socialism is not just about currency; it's an ideology that convinces us that others are responsible for us and our success. Socialism and entitlement are the outcome of abdicating our destiny and placing it into the hands of a system rather than a supernatural Father, who is willing to break into our God-dreams and give us supernatural power to fly above the storms and overcome life's obstacles.

Those who have eyes to see will lift their vision and be on the cutting edge of change while accusers sit around and mourn the loss of "Egypt's comforts." How smart is it to look to a worldly system for answers and then be surprised that its answers contain only the opinions of the world, and lack heaven's genuine solutions? As forward-thinking as the western-world may be, It is still having trouble paying it's own debt, it is still practicing medicine, and many of its politicians have partnered with the media to lead us into another civil war. What the world needs is only found in the supernatural realm. Why are we trying to change a worldly system with worldly antidotes when heaven's culture, which is not of this world, is the ONLY answer to solve earth's problems? We will see the Daniels and Josephs who think on an entirely different supernatural plane begin to rise up. It's often too easy to sit in the judgement seat as an "arm-chair quarterback" and tell society what they are not doing. We need people who hear from heaven and release solutions. Joseph did not have to dishonor Pharaoh to bring the kingdom; Daniel did not have to dishonor Nebuchadnezzar. They both possessed the heart of a servant and used supernatural wisdom and revelation that was so undeniably powerful it was irrefutable.

God is releasing a company of "next generation" wrecking balls in the mountain of politics. They are heaven's answer sent to counterattack the spirit of socialism. They will model kingdom success and create policies that cause nations to thrive in a free-market and fair-trade society. I believe that God is already tugging on the heart of some of Donald Trump's children, as well as others, to be a big part of this revolution. Much of what King David was called to accomplish happened through his son Solomon. I believe that there is still much that God has for Donald Trump Sr. to accomplish, but look for his legacy to be passed down early. His children are called to be true patriots and will be agents of change.

Transformational Drivers

I believe that God is releasing grace to focus on four primary drivers for global transformation. These four important keys are necessary to establish kingdom culture on the earth. They are not the only drivers for transformation, but they are among the top priorities of heaven that God plans to leverage for His purpose on the earth.

- Apostolic Resource Centers
- Capitalization
- Media
- Technology

Apostolic Resource Centers (ARC's) will be established in many regions across the globe as kingdom embassies that have their finger on the pulse of the heart of God, and are aware of what their regions individually need to prosper. These ARC's will mobilize a company of people who intentionally love and serve their regions well. They will have credibility in the gates of their regions because they have served them without agenda and have gained influence. They are being positioned to overtly solve the most pressing problems and promote the name of Jesus as their only agenda. They will change the definition of how the world sees the church in one generation. They will launch initiatives that create resources out of what seems to be problems. They will hear from heaven and receive high-level revelations that solve crimes, release new technology, fund kingdom initiatives, mobilize God's people to serve, and release signs, wonders, and miracles to reveal the presence of God in these regions around the globe. They will set the bar for a new breed of Christianity and will be located strategically around the world.

Capitalization models for funding your God-dream are being released from heaven in this hour. Up to this point, much of the nonprofit world has operated primarily from the donor model. This model may remain intact, but new forms of capitalization will now begin to arise. While individuals suffering from a "slave mentality" would face the temptation to not be good stewards of kingdom wealth, God is about to trust high levels of capital to His sons and daughters. Having the ability to clearly articulate vision and goals will also be crucial in this time. God will give you favor with financiers, but they will not dig into their deep pockets to help fund your God-dream unless you have your POC (proof of concept) well beyond the dreaming stage. These wealthy individuals and venture capital groups are already good stewards of wealth and they have a keen ability to recognize those who have thoroughly developed their process. You will need to have your "elevator speech" ready—your two-minute opportunity where the Lord can arrest the hearts of people with the vision He has placed inside of you. This is your Habakkuk 2 call: "write down the vision and make it plain so that he who reads it may run with it." Make sure that you have the "why, who, and how" of your vision distilled into a two minute, passion-filled conversation, be able to articulate what problems your ideas solve, and be ready to share your POC; what has worked for you and what has not. Wealth will come to those who will use it for kingdom purposes. This wealth transfer into your hands will not only fund your personal vision but is meant to also fund the vision of your local church, and initiatives for the end-time global harvest.

Media will continue to be the arena for the battle to shape culture's narrative. Will God's people use this platform to create an atmosphere of hope or will fear prevail and shape the conscience of the masses? Social reformers are being released by the Lord with the understanding that their mandate is to use this platform for kingdom purposes. If you want to bring transformation to any region you have to begin by establishing kingdom language. History has shown that dictators understand this concept and have used propaganda to create fear in the hearts of the people, so that the dictator can set themselves up to be the rescuer. God cares about His life-giving language dominating the airwaves. This same kind of revolution began in the upper room in the first century when the church was launched. When the Holy Spirit fell, Christians received more than the gift of tongues; they received the gift of articulation. This is the supernatural ability to release the glories and strategies of heaven to someone who doesn't understand Christian-ese. Media will be used by the Holy Spirit to create the narrative for every nation on earth.

Technology is a main driver for transformation because it creates a tangible platform for heaven's ideas to manifest. Every sphere of society is affected by technology in large and small ways. To avoid having influence in this mountain would create the same scenario as abdicating our kingdom role in the political arena. The absence would be devastating and would create a huge pit that the next generation of Christians will have to dig their way out of. Technology is a platform that God leverages to shout to the world that His thoughts are higher than ours. His ways are not irrelevant, but are wise, loving, and just, capable of causing society in every nation on the entire globe to flourish. Breakthrough discoveries in space and on the earth are about to be released and it is time that the church is overt and ready to reveal that God is the source behind their genius.

He is the most forward-thinking, the most brilliant and innovative Creator ever known. He is about to flex His muscles and shout to get our attention. Then we will live in the awareness of His constant presence without fear and we will see Him set Himself as the Great God, just like He did in Isaiah 44:8:

> "Do not tremble, do not be afraid. Did I not proclaim this and foretell it long ago? You are my witnesses. Is there any God besides me? No, there is no other Rock; I know not one."

Authority Over Chaos

We are about to get an upgrade! We are about to be washed in the water of the Word of God Himself, like never before, through the release of revelatory grace on the teaching anointing. We will tremble as His Word comes alive to us and we find ourselves in His story. Fiery men and women will carry and release revelation that arrests the hearts of men; that provides refreshing living water that quenches the thirst of those who understand that we are parched and desperate, and that there is more that we have yet to experience in God. This will help us to set our minds on things above. We need a revolution of maturity. We need to revolt against self-centeredness and carnality and see that our role as Christians is to bring a supernatural kingdom to this planet. We need to exchange our accusations for innovation and begin to show the world that we are immune to its chaos. We are rolling up our sleeves, getting involved, and living lives that provoke people to godly jealousy and their desperate need for Jesus.

> God is about to flex His muscles and shout to get our attention. Then we will live in the awareness of His constant presence without fear.

> "I leave the gift of peace with you—my peace. Not the kind of fragile peace given by the world, but my perfect peace. Don't yield to fear or be troubled in your hearts—instead, be courageous!" (John 14:27, TPT)

One of the last things that Jesus imparted to His disciples was the reality of this John 14:27 anointing, which is the anointing to release "authority over chaos." The word "peace" in this verse comes from the Hebrew word shalom, which means "authority over chaos." He has given us this anointing to release His peace wherever fear or chaos manifests. You will not only experience high realities of peace in this hour, like never before, you will exercise authority over the chaos of this world as you release the influence of the Prince of Peace wherever you go.

KATHI PELTON

Kathi Pelton is an author and prophetic voice to the church. She and her husband Jeffrey walk with nations and individuals to see God's original intent fulfilled. Their ministry, Inscribe Ministries, was founded upon the verse from Habakkuk 2:2, *Then the LORD answered me and said: "Write the vision and make it plain on tablets, that he may run who reads it."*

Kathi has served on the leadership team for Watchmen for the Nations for many years, and she is also a frequent contributor to The Elijah List and many other prophetic publications.

She and Jeffrey have four adult children and three grandchildren.

9
A WRESTLE, OR A DANCE?
Kathi Pelton

If we are to understand what is to come in 2021 and beyond, we must first understand the significance of 2020.

This past year was truly an unprecedented time of global and national shakings, trials, and clashes. Yet, amid a world in chaos, God's remnant was awakening into a oneness with God and one another like never before.

The scripture that the Lord gave me the end of last year, just before crossing into 2020, was from Zechariah 4:6:

> So he said to me, "This is the word of the Lord to Zerubbabel: 'Not by might nor by power, but by my Spirit,' says the Lord Almighty."

I experienced deep sobriety regarding the Lord's desire to move us, His *ekklesia*, as well as the people of our nation (the United States of America), from reliance on *our might and strength to full dependency upon His Spirit*. I had little idea how true this would prove to be.

In the first months of the year, as we watched the cancelation of multiple stadium events that we believed would be the threshing floor of a great harvest, we truly had no idea that 2020 was a year to be prepared for that harvest. The previous years had prepared us for a return to First Love. Now, we watched as churches emptied due to Covid-19, businesses closed, face-to-face fellowship ceased, and the whole world shut down. There was nothing we could do but lean on the Holy Spirit and use this time to go deeper into the presence of God than we had ever gone before.

In March 2020, I had a powerful visionary encounter that revealed great understanding of what the Lord was desiring. In this encounter I saw Jesus knock on the door of his bride's heart. She quickly and excitedly opened the door to her Beloved. But he could not enter because there was so much clutter scattered across the floor. I was interested to see that the clutter was mostly spiritual things that might be valuable, but they were unnecessary for the time ahead. I saw books, teachings, notes, formulas for specific ways to pray, and so much more. All that the bride had learned in the past was stacked throughout this room of her heart.

Jesus asked, "Can I make room in your heart for me?"

Immediately, she responded sincerely, "Yes, my heart belongs to you, Lord." The Lord began to clear her heart of the mounds of clutter, but she was astonished when, instead of neatly stacking and reordering her piles of possessions, he emptied the room of everything. He then carried in a modest wooden table and two chairs, placed a loaf of bread and a cup of wine on the table, and sat down. As he settled in his chair, he motioned to the other one and said, *"Come and sit with me. Everything you need is here."*

Over the next months, I spent many days dwelling with him in the room of my heart. He taught me new insights about his body, his blood, his longings, his presence, and his love. Everything became so simple and yet so profound. I understood that He was taking us back to the message of the finished work of the cross where love triumphed over death and hell. I knew this was the message that would bring a great harvest of souls into his kingdom.

Before this sovereign and "set apart" time forced upon us this year, our intentions and our message had become too convoluted for the lost to understand. We had become wise in our own eyes, while having lost the beautiful message of salvation by grace, the power of the cross, the resurrection, and the Lord's ascension to be seated at the right hand of his Father.

> After the Lord Jesus had spoken to them, He was taken up into heaven and sat down at the right hand of God. And they went out and preached everywhere, and the Lord worked through them, confirming His word by the signs that accompanied it. (Mark 16:19-20)

I have heard believers ask, "Where is the power to heal and deliver?" Our answer has been to go to classes, conferences, and schools that taught us how to address these issues in prayer. They have not been unhelpful or ineffective, but I believe we are moving into an era where our preaching will be confirmed by signs and wonders.

Toward the end of 2020 I had the privilege of leading a lady to Jesus who had been violently molested and violated as a child during her years in the foster care system. She needed salvation but she also needed deliverance from tormenting spirits and from deep roots of bitterness. I laid hands on her and prayed a simple prayer from my heart for God to come and wash over her and resurrect her from the grave she had been living in. She hugged me and wept in my arms as she told Jesus she wanted to know him and live in freedom.

I gave her my contact information before I left, and within ten minutes of driving away I began to receive texts from her saying how suddenly her hands began to shake and love poured into her like she had never experienced. As this happened, she felt demons leaving her, and peace washed over her for the first time in her life. She wrote only Jesus was with her. Power, signs and wonders had followed our simple encounter, and this precious lady was delivered without anyone present but the Holy Spirit. I believe that this is a foretaste of what we will see in 2021 and beyond. People will get saved and delivered in a moment and begin praising God.

But first, we needed the clutter removed so we could return to our first love and the simple truth of the gospel.

> For the word of the cross is folly to those who are perishing, but to us who are being saved it is the power of God. (1 Corinthians 1:18)

The cross will once again be recognized as the true power to save, heal, and deliver as this great harvest comes in. We will not need to rely upon methods, formulas, or even the *good* teachings of man, because the harvest will be happening so fast we will need his power to accompany salvation, so that the saved immediately begin preaching what they have just received. His Word will be alive and moving in power once again through us as the church returns to the finished work of the cross.

The church and the enemies of God will see manifestations of his might, his power, and his sovereignty.

> He himself bore our sins in his body on the tree, that we might die to sin and live to righteousness. By his wounds you have been healed. (1 Peter 2:24)

We Will Be One in 2021

For more than twenty years I have been praying the words from the last recorded prayer of Jesus found in John 17:20-23,

> My prayer is not for them alone. I pray also for those who will believe in me through their message, that all of them may be one, Father, just as you are in me and I am in you. May they also be in us so that the world

> may believe that you have sent me. I have given them the glory that you gave me, that they may be one as we are one— I in them and you in me—so that they may be brought to complete unity. Then the world will know that you sent me and have loved them even as you have loved me.

The prayer of Jesus, joined by multitudes of believers around the world, was revealed in a greater way than I have ever seen before in 2020. Who would have guessed that in a time of global separation we would see the global body of Christ become more unified then we have ever seen in history?

First, God used our separation and quarantine to bring us into oneness with him as we allowed him to take us into deep refinement, repentance, and restoration to first love.

Then, as no one was able to travel we turned to Zoom calls to connect, pray together, share our longings and desires, and fight for one another. Suddenly strangers were not only friends, but family, as people across the globe were invited into our homes. Nations began to stand with nations, and we fell in love with each another, ushering deep repentance and healing to the places where divisions once separated us.

I believe that 2021 will prove to be the beginning of walking out oneness. John 17 says that when we become one with God and enter complete unity, then the world will know that the Father sent the Son and has loved them EVEN AS HE HAS LOVED HIS OWN SON! The power of the revelation of the Father's love will restore identity, bring the lonely into family, and cause orphans to become sons and daughters.

> For God so loved the world that he gave his one and only Son, that whoever believes in him shall not perish but have eternal life. (John 3:16)

How could the Father give his only Son unless he loved us even as he loves his own Son? We were created to be his sons and daughters! He does not love us any less than he loves his only Son. And—the Son loves us equally as much as the Father because they are one. And—the Spirit fully shares the Father's and the Son's love for us. Remarkably, we are invited into the oneness of that unbroken love and communion. Amid a world burdened by broken families and confused identity, we will extend an invitation for those who have not known true love to come into a family that is whole and full of agape love. This will blow away the fog of confusion about identity, causing divine deliverance to come upon those who accept the invitation into God's family. Their constant search for identity will end as they look into the face of God and his image is restored to them. They will suddenly know who they are as they receive revelation of who he is. Sounds of deliverance will resound throughout the world.

2021 will be marked with oneness! I believe this oneness will cause the ecclesia to shine with a light that draws men to Christ in a way we have yet to experience. We will not be spending exorbitant amounts of time trying to convince people of the love of God because they will see it in our unity; many will come without a word being spoken.

A Year to Occupy

We have learned to war, but 2021 begins our strategies of occupation. When we gain victories, we must then occupy the land we have won. God will teach the body of Christ how to occupy the ground we have taken through our warring.

The final months of 2020 have taught God's remnant to take their seats of authority in heavenly places with Christ. A revelation of the authority given to us in Christ Jesus will usher in victories that write hope for the future on the blank pages of days to come.

And God raised us up with Christ and seated us with

> him in the heavenly realms in Christ Jesus, in order that in the coming ages he might show the incomparable riches of his grace, expressed in his kindness to us in Christ Jesus. (Ephesians 2:6-7)

God has put his remnant in their heavenly sets of government, and now they will rule and reign with him like never in history. When Jesus ascended to his throne, we ascended into a place of authority with him. Now we will occupy our seats and exercise our spiritual authority on earth as it is in heaven!

This will be a year to sit in the seats of victory that were gained in 2020. It is time to occupy our seats in heavenly places, as well as a time where more of God's people will be called to occupy seats of earthly government. We will see the emergence of godly governmental leaders standing for righteousness, calling their nations to return to God.

God's government has been called into session for such a time as this. The Lord's scepter has been extended; it is a year to decree, a year to exercise authority, a year to rule from the seats of spiritual authority. We will see the formation of a spiritual "United Nations" begin to manifest that will rule and reign with Christ Jesus.

America will no longer stand alone but will stand as one with the ecclesia throughout the nations to decree righteousness, justice, and liberty in Jesus. Together we will raise the standard of the Lord over America and over the nations. We will occupy the land that we have warred for in 2020. The Lord is saying, "Take your seats, children of God! Touch the scepter and release the decree that delivers the nations of the world."

> Esther said, "If it please the king, and if I have found favor with him, and if he thinks it is right, and if I am pleasing to him, let there be a decree that reverses the orders of Haman son of Hammedatha the Agagite, who ordered that Jews throughout all the king's provinces should be

destroyed. For how can I endure to see my people and my family slaughtered and destroyed?" (Esther 8:5-6)

This will be a year of the King's scepter. As his ecclesia has crowned him King of the Universe and his bride has taken her place next to him, we will decree deliverance to the seven mountains of influence through the cultures of the world. We have been invited to approach him, and to take our place next to him and reign with him. 2021 will be known as a "for such a time as this" point in history; a time to occupy and decree!

The Crown of Authority and The Signet Ring
During the Rosh Hashanah seasons of 2019 and 2020 I had two encounters that I believe it is important to take note of. In 2019 I awoke one morning hearing the words, *"It's coronation day!"* I was shown a clear vision of Jesus crowning his bride as his queen. She was then seated in her place of authority next to her Bridegroom.

The following year, during Rosh Hashanah 2020, I once again awoke hearing similar words but this time it was, *"Coronation of the Son."* I immediately was taken to Psalm 2 where I read,

> Why do the nations conspire
> and the peoples plot in vain?
> The kings of the earth rise up
> and the rulers band together
> against the Lord and against his anointed, saying,
> "Let us break their chains
> and throw off their shackles."
>
> The One enthroned in heaven laughs;
> the Lord scoffs at them.
> He rebukes them in his anger
> and terrifies them in his wrath, saying,
> "I have installed my king
> on Zion, my holy mountain."

> I will proclaim the LORD's decree:
>
> He said to me, "You are my son;
> today I have become your father.
> Ask me,
> and I will make the nations your inheritance,
> the ends of the earth your possession.
> You will break them with a rod of iron;
> you will dash them to pieces like pottery."
>
> Therefore, you kings, be wise;
> be warned, you rulers of the earth.
> Serve the LORD with fear
> and celebrate his rule with trembling.
> Kiss his son, or he will be angry
> and your way will lead to your destruction,
> for his wrath can flare up in a moment.
> Blessed are all who take refuge in him.

During Rosh Hashanah I became aware that there was a declaration of Jesus being our crowned King. "No King but Jesus" was on the tongue of countless believers, and I was privileged to witness several gatherings of the *ecclesia* crowing Christ as their king.

During this time, while on a prayer assignment in Washington D.C. (we live in the D.C. region), the Holy Spirit asked me to wear my wedding ring. This might not sound unusual, but the diamond in my wedding ring had fallen out twenty years earlier and I have never had it replaced. The Lord asked me to wear a ring that had no diamond. I had not put it on my finger in over twenty years. When I asked him about it, he responded, "Today I will join the ring with a diamond as a sign that I am giving the church my signet ring."

Toward the end of our prayer assignment one of the ladies with us glanced at the ground and in the mud near her feet was a large diamond! I was wearing the wedding band and she discovered the diamond. As she picked it up and cleaned it off, I heard Haggai 2:21-23:

"Tell Zerubbabel governor of Judah that I am going to shake the heavens and the earth. I will overturn royal thrones and shatter the power of the foreign kingdoms. I will overthrow chariots and their drivers; horses and their riders will fall, each by the sword of his brother.

"'On that day,' declares the LORD Almighty, 'I will take you, my servant Zerubbabel son of Shealtiel,' declares the LORD, 'and I will make you like my signet ring, for I have chosen you,' declares the LORD Almighty."

He truly is confirming his word in sovereign encounters as we walk in humble obedience.

A Holy Revolution

A spiritual revolutionary war has begun to set us free from demonic rule, establishing the Lord's rule in the United States and other nations. I believe that the end of 2020 has brought the United States to a time similar to the events in December 1776, when George Washington crossed the Delaware River on Christmas day to give the Continental Army its first victory in the Revolutionary War.

Washington had planned to cross the Delaware at night to launch a surprise attack against a garrison of enemy troops stationed in Trenton, New Jersey. The river was frozen, and the conditions were so harsh that though Washington's attack was to comprise three separate crossings, only one out of three could cross—and the successful vessel contained George Washington himself. Prior to the crossing, Washington's carefully planned timetable was so badly behind schedule because of the weather that he contemplated canceling the attack.

> **We will raise the standard of the Lord over the nations. We will occupy the land that we have warred for in 2020.**

Across the river, a spy had warned the British army that this surprise attack would take place, but the commanding general was arrogant and believed it to be another "false alarm," so he did not prepare his troops. Washington's crossing and surprise attack secured the Continental Army's first major military victory of the Revolutionary War. The courageous decision by General Washington was clearly a "succeed or die" scenario.

The courage given to George Washington in this perilous time will come upon the church repeatedly in 2021. We will be filled with boldness and courage to cross many rivers and gain victory in many battles. The Lord showed me men like Moses, Joshua, and Caleb who stood before rivers that were impossible to cross, but as they put their faith in the *God of Impossibilities* the waters parted and his people crossed over on dry land. 2020 was like crossing the Jordan River and now it is time for us to take our land of promise flowing with milk and honey. There will be many battles ahead, but if we listen to God's instructions and keep his ways, we will be victorious and occupy the land. It is important to keep our eyes on the immensity of God rather than the size of the giants who oppose us. I hear the words from Job 26 resounding in 2021:

> "The realm of the dead is naked before God;
>   Destruction lies uncovered.
> He spreads out the northern skies over empty space;
>   he suspends the earth over nothing.
> He wraps up the waters in his clouds,
>   yet the clouds do not burst under their weight.
> He covers the face of the full moon,
>   spreading his clouds over it.
> He marks out the horizon on the face of the waters
>   for a boundary between light and darkness.
> The pillars of the heavens quake,
>   aghast at his rebuke.
> By his power he churned up the sea;

> by his wisdom he cut Rahab to pieces.
> By his breath the skies became fair;
>   his hand pierced the gliding serpent.
> And these are but the outer fringe of his works;
>   how faint the whisper we hear of him!
> Who then can understand the thunder of his power?"

The church and the enemies of God will see manifestations of his might, his power, and his sovereignty. We will see the rod of Moses part seas, and we will see the Rod of Jesse free his people from captivity, oppression, and tyranny (Isaiah 11:1-5). There will be great battles, but even greater, miraculous victories that cause his people to rejoice with all their hearts. No man will take credit for the victories we will begin to see in 2021. The children born in this hour will be filled with faith and will understand the power and sovereignty of God, because they are being raised in an era known for the display of his power and might!

My Most Important Word for 2021: A Wrestle or A Dance

As I write this, we are in the final weeks of 2020. I recently had an encounter with the Lord regarding 2021 and beyond that was simple yet profound. One day in prayer I heard the words, *"It will be either a wrestle or a dance."*

Then I saw a vision of Jesus inviting his people to dance with him. I knew that he had been teaching his remnant to move in step with him in a new way during 2020. A plumbline had dropped, and his remnant has been aligning to the standards of his love and sovereignty. As we enter 2021 it will be vitally important to "let him lead." The dance will be intimate, face-to-face, and hand-in-hand, but we must learn to match our steps to his. I heard the Lord say, **"Don't look at your feet, but look in my eyes and your feet will follow."** As we keep our eyes fixed upon his, our feet will easily follow his lead.

Then I saw others who insisted on functioning the way they always had in years past. They were still trying to take the lead in their walk with God, in family, in ministry, in business, and in government. They immediately began stepping on Jesus's feet and getting all tangled up in his steps. What was designed to be a dance suddenly became a wrestle.

In the season to come, the path will become much harder to follow for those who do not draw near and let the Lord guide their every step.

As this book was going to print, I had an encounter about the Lord's dominion and heard "Dominion Dance." I saw the *ekklesia* declaring Jesus's dominion and crowning Him with worship. I also understood that the enemy seeks to usurp "dominion" on the earth. But the dance we have been invited into is one where every move declares "He shall have dominion from sea to sea!" This resounds throughout the earth as the Lord's people declare it with every movement, and heaven and earth hear that all dominion belongs to Yahweh alone. This dance will defeat the dominion that satan desires to presumptuously assert for himself. Our steps will trample every demonic "dominion" and exalt the only true King!

It is time to choose the dance and let him lead. It is time to draw near—take his hand and fix your eyes upon his—and let the dance begin.

> Therefore, since we are surrounded by such a great cloud of witnesses, let us throw off everything that hinders and the sin that so easily entangles. And let us run with perseverance the race marked out for us, fixing our eyes on Jesus, the pioneer and perfecter of faith. For the joy set before him he endured the cross, scorning its shame, and sat down at the right hand of the throne of God. (Hebrews 12:1-2)

Daneen Bottler

Daneen Bottler is a dynamic prophetic voice for this generation. She carries a Kingdom mandate to release her prophetic voice to bring awakening to the body of Christ and train up a prophetic generation that will rise up into all they were created to be, extending and demonstrating the Kingdom of God in authority and power. Daneen and her husband Ty live in Portland, Oregon along with their two children Trenton and Kylie, where they serve as the Executive and Worship Pastors of Father's House City Ministries. Daneen and Ty have had the privilege of speaking and ministering at various churches, conferences, and schools throughout the United States and Canada.

Daneen has written for The Elijah List and other prophetic publications.

10
CROSSING THE THRESHOLD
Daneen Bottler

In the fall of 2020, the Holy Spirit began to speak to me about what He was going to do in 2021. As I pressed in to hear what He would say, the Lord began to show me pictures and give me dreams and impressions about what was to come. All these interactions with the Holy Spirit centered on one overarching theme: the absolute Supremacy of the Lord Jesus Christ over all things. While I was aware of many timelines interwoven within this narrative of our victorious King, in 2021, there will be an exclamation point demonstrated by the Lord and played out before the nations. The Lord spoke to me very clearly, "Daneen, the sound of the hour is the sound of my power!" It was an emphatic statement. The power of God has a sound. Psalm 29:4-5 says,

> The voice of the Lord is powerful, the voice of the Lord is majestic. The voice of the Lord breaks the cedars, Yes the Lord breaks in pieces the cedars of Lebanon.

This great show of God's power will herald the beginning of the great harvesting age in the Kingdom and on the earth. Just like the showdown on Mt. Carmel between Elijah and the prophets of Baal, there will be a demonstration of God's power that awakens the people and the nations out of their slumber, bringing them into the glorious light of Christ; a show of power that brings finality to the showdown between the false gods of the United States of America and the Lord Almighty, ending with the verdict that Jesus Christ is the one, true, supreme God. In 2021 we will see these words from the apostle Paul become a standard waved from even the highest court in the land:

> Therefore, God elevated him to the place of highest honor and gave him the name above all other names, that at the name of Jesus every knee should bow, in heaven and on earth and under the earth, and every tongue declare that Jesus Christ is Lord, to the glory of God the Father. (Philippians 2:9-11)

Jesus Christ is the Alpha and The Omega, the First and the Last. He is El Elyon, the Supreme One, God Most High. In Jesus, there is no shadow of turning, nor is darkness found anywhere in Him. I want to be very clear when releasing this prophetic word, so the reader understands that I am not prophesying that this is "the End," or that an apocalypse is about to happen. However, 2020 marks the end of a literal forty-year period that brings a deliverance cycle into completion in the United States and the body of Christ at large. I am trying to bring understanding that in our current time period, the Lord is choosing to move into our chronological timeline, and through His people, thwart the plans of the wicked, subdue the nations that have turned against Him, and realign the United States of America to His original intent and heart for her. But this will require the bride of Christ to walk across the threshold with her Bridegroom as her one and only true love.

The Threshold and Threshing Floor

While 2020 showed us the door to the new era that will bring us into a decade of roaring twenties, 2021 is the transition period between the two eras. 2021 will require the church to walk across the threshold into the new. The word "threshold" represents the idea of transition, of moving across and arriving from outside a door into wherever the doorway leads. It signifies the beginning of forward motion. As we move from 2020 into 2021, what happens in the transition will indicate the pace of our forward momentum into the new era. Everything that can be shaken is being shaken in order to produce the necessary shifts in our paradigms and ways. Our thinking must be renewed in Christ Jesus and our ways must become His ways once more. It will require many structures, practices and traditional understandings to be left at the foot of the cross to move into the new.

> The Lord spoke to me clearly, "Daneen, the sound of the hour is the sound of my power!"

In Matthew chapter thirteen, we see that John the Baptist is baptizing for the repentance of sins. John begins to talk about the One who would come after him, speaking of Jesus. In verse twelve, John makes a very important statement:

> "He will baptize you with the Holy Spirit and fire, His **winnowing fork** is in His hand, and He will thoroughly clear His threshing floor: and He will gather His wheat into the barn, but He will burn up the chaff with unquenchable fire."
> (Matthew 3:12, emphasis mine)

The body of Christ is being called to the threshing floor so the Lord can thresh us, so we will surrender to Him fully and let Him separate the grain stocks from the wheat in us. There is a call to complete and total surrender to the Lord, to trust Him fully, even as Job stated, "If he slay me, yet I will trust him."

Old ways cannot create or produce new results. New ways, specifically God's ways, are required for us to flourish in the new era. This year will be a year of surrendering the old ways and understandings in order to receive fresh revelation and vision for what we have moved into. In plain-speak, it will mean a lot of dying to "self," taking up our cross and coming alive to Christ Jesus—in our own personal lives as well as in the church at large. There are many thousands of churches that have been built, but not many where the glory of God is truly dwelling. There are many believers who have become disillusioned, jaded, and embittered because God is not moving the way they want or how they think He should. These types of personal agendas, strongholds, and wrong perspectives have to be dealt with in the body of Christ before they can be dealt with in the world. Judgement first comes to the house of the Lord. God is calling His house into order. He is calling his people to repent and turn back to Him with their whole hearts, to realign their hearts with His and receive a fresh baptism into His fire and love. The mountain of the Lord is to become the chief of the mountains. He who has ears to hear, let him hear what the Spirit is saying!

The Holy Spirit said to me, "The year 2021 is not only a threshold year, but is to become the threshing floor." This coming year will be a year of great purification and consecration in the house of God, for God is coming to baptize his bride in his fire. The church has tolerated perversion and witchcraft far too long. We have become passive in our commission and settled for programs and theatrical performances instead of asking for the fire of God to consume us and His holy presence to inhabit us. We desperately need the passionate fire of God to overwhelm us, that we would be changed into different men and women. Instead, we have gotten fat and over-spiritualized, and the message of consecration, holiness, and righteousness have left the church building. God is raising up a remnant of laid-down lovers of Jesus, filled with his fire to walk in His power, just as Jesus did on earth. Demonstrations of God's power only move through lives that have been consecrated and walk humbly before Him.

2020 was a year of upheaval as life the way it has always been was blown out of the water and replaced with uncertainty. Opposition appeared to challenge the status quo and we saw a spirit of insanity grip the earth. These events, and many others, which appeared as opposition and obstacles were actually opportunities in disguise, but many Christians did not see it that way. Instead, many grew discouraged and weary as the battle raged on. As their eyes came off Jesus and onto the circumstances, many believers entered a deep, dark valley, where their faith in the Lord was tested. I heard the Lord say, "I Am your deliver. What was the like the valley of the shadow of death has now become the valley of decision." 2021 will bring with it deliverance from the enemy, but as with every deliverance that occurs, there is a choice to be made as to whom you will serve. This choice is dealing with the realm of Lordship in your life. In the book of Joshua, Joshua says to the people,

> "Choose you this day whom you will serve…but as for me and my household, we will serve the Lord." (Joshua 24:15, my paraphrase)

The Israelites found serving the Lord disagreeable and wanted to serve the false gods of the Amorites. There are many idols and false gods looking to draw our devotion and desires, but we must be those who decide once and for all that we will serve the Lord! This means even if I don't especially feel like it, I will set my will on the Lord; if I think something is unfair, still I will choose to set my will to serve the Lord; if something that seems negative happens to me or my family, still I will choose to set my will to serve the Lord. This is where we must be. WE CHOOSE TO SERVE THE LORD WITH OUR WHOLE HEARTS.

The Lord is saying to His people, "Choose you this day, whom you will serve. Let your choice be made evident to all. To serve Me, requires a covenant that refuses idolatry of any kind. For I am a jealous God! I am jealous for My bride."

In another chapter of the book of Joshua, we find Joshua has a poignant encounter with an angel that is relevant to 2021.

> Now it came about when Joshua was by Jericho, he raised his eyes and looked, and behold, a man was standing opposite him with his sword drawn in his hand, and Joshua went to him and said to him, "Are you for us or for our enemies?" He said, "No; rather I have come now as captain of the army of the Lord." And Joshua fell on his face to the ground, and bowed down, and said to him, "What has my lord to say to his servant?" And the captain of the Lord's army said to Joshua, "Remove your sandals from your feet, for the place where you are standing is holy." And Joshua did so. (Joshua 5:13-15)

What we see in this passage of Scripture is that the Lord appears to Joshua as captain of the Lord's army. Joshua doesn't recognize him and asks this all-important question, "Are you for us or for our enemies?" In other words, Joshua is asking the angel, whose side are you on? But look at the Lord's response to Joshua, "NO." No what? The answer is no, the angel was not on any human's side, but rather: "I am the captain of the Lord's army."

What the angel is saying to Joshua here is that He, the angel, is on the Lord's side. This causes Joshua to fall face down and ask what the Lord has to say to him. Joshua recognized that instead of getting the angel on his side, Joshua needed to be on God's side.

This is what God will be doing in 2021. He will show up and we will be faced with the choice: are we going to get on His side, or are we going to do our own thing? Being on God's side means that God is going to do things God's way, regardless of whether it fits in our boxes or aligns with our perspectives, and we are going to choose to align our hearts, churches, families, regions, and nations to His ways. Jesus is looking for His church, His ecclesia, to get on His side. God is not taking any man's side. The question that is to be answered in 2021 is, whose side are we on?

The Winnowing

As we move into 2021 we will begin to see a great winnowing happen in the church. Winnowing is a harvesting term that speaks of the wind separating the dust from the head of wheat. Biblically, there are many metaphors that God uses to describe His separating and dividing out the truth from counterfeit, good from evil, saved from unsaved. One such metaphor is the winnowing of the wheat and the chaff. Chaff represents those things that hold the appearance of being genuine, but are in reality just a hollow façade. In 2021 God will lead us into the process of separating those who are not actually following him from those who are. It is Jesus Christ Himself who is the great divider.

> "Do not think that I came to bring peace on the earth; I did not come to [aa]bring peace, but a sword. For I came to turn a man against his father, and a daughter against her mother, and a daughter-in-law against her mother-in-law; and a person's enemies will be the members of his household.
> "The one who loves father or mother more than Me is not worthy of Me; and the one who loves son or daughter more than Me is not worthy of Me. And the one who does not take his cross and follow after Me is not worthy of Me. The one who has found his life will lose it, and the one who has lost his life on My account will find it. " (Matthew 10:34-37)

Churches were not meant to be institutions, but instead the church is meant to be an instrument of God's power in the earth, displaying His radiant glory. In 2021 we will see the beginning of a mass dividing and separating in the church. Individuals who are hungering and thirsting for righteousness, for the living God, those who will lay down their lives for the sake of the upward calling in Christ Jesus, these will begin to exit the buildings that are dead inside, to find other groups moving according to the leading of the Holy Spirit. As we move into this new era, there will be a definite divide between churches ruled by Christ Jesus, the Head of the body, where God is present and operating in power, versus churches ruled by man, where the religious spirit, political spirit, perversion, and witchcraft reign, causing them to become graveyards devoid of God's power and presence. Neither the religious nor political spirit will conform to anything that does not satisfy itself or bring self-gain. Where the religious spirit reigns, the Holy Spirit is quenched. God is ready to see His bride come to life carrying the fire that is in His eyes and becoming the instrument of His power on the earth. This is her call; this is her destiny. This great purification and winnowing is happening so that the church will become the sign and wonder to the world around her. She is part of God's demonstration of power, but for that power to be released, the threshing and winnowing must occur.

> Churches were not meant to be institutions, but instead the church is meant to be an instrument of God's power in the earth, displaying His radiant glory.

It would be easy for me to give a flowery word and gloss over the requirements for advancement, but it would not be the Word of the Lord. The Word of the Lord comes not only to encourage and equip us for the days ahead, but also to correct our course and direct our feet to where the Spirit is leading. Let the reader understand that we are in a most important and crucial time in history. God's ways, God's wisdom, and God's laws are perfect. We must be vigilant in keeping our eyes on the author and finisher of our faith. There is a time and season under heaven for everything. We have entered into a time that requires us to be focused, alert, and engaged, not messing about and playing at church. We must set our hearts to seeking the Lord in fervent faith, believing that not only does He hear us when we pray, but that He is delighted to answer us and show us the way of wisdom and where to walk.

God is revealing His majesty and supremacy in both power and authority. In the last few years we have been in a showdown for not only the soul of the United States of America, but the souls of the nations of the world. Just like in the story of Elijah, we have seen the false prophets of the enemy carrying on and doing their best to invoke the power of false gods in our country. They are sacrificing children, shedding innocent blood, attempting to villainize good by calling it evil, and heralding wickedness and sexual perversion as righteousness, all in an attempt to enthrone their false gods in the U.S.

As a prophet of the Most High, I am telling you that God has had enough of the rebellion and workers of iniquity. Their practices have risen like a stench in his nostrils. Elohei Mishpat, the God of Justice, is on the move. He has heard the cries of the righteous in this nation. He has seen the tears shed as the saints of God have stood in the place of repentance for their sins and cried out to the Lord for his mercy. The blood of Jesus speaks a better word. It cleanses even the land from sin and iniquity. In every deliverance story from the Old Testament to the New, God always establishes His absolute supremacy over every false god of the oppressing or usurping nations. A revealing of the omnipotent God Most High is what always sent terror into the heart of Israel's enemies and as the saints continue to cry out, continue to intercede, continue to pray for the United State of America, this revealing of Jesus Christ as the Supreme God is what will start to begin to be established in 2021.

The Media Mountain

The cultural mountain of media, which has been aligned with the enemy's narrative, trumpeting falsehoods and perversion, will now begin to shift. I hear the Lord saying that in 2021 there is coming a shake-up and a shake-down to the cultural mountain of media. For the Lord has judged the false prophets of the media and he is going to bring a firestorm of His truth and the execution of His righteous judgment upon it. This year there will be an exposing of the workers of iniquity specifically within the media mountain. People who have been party to backhanded deals for power will be exposed. People who did nothing when they knew that slander and injustice was being perpetrated on the innocent, people who hid in the dark, will be brought into the light. We will see heads of news organizations fired, and in some cases legal charges brought against them and the top leadership. I saw a picture of certain well-known news agencies filing for bankruptcy because the Lord is humbling them in the sight of the nations. The truth of the Lord will prevail and this cultural mountain will see a stripping begin this year. The ears of people will no longer be tuned into the news media for truth because their lies and deceptions will be exposed. God will bring an opportunity for the rebuilding of the platform of this mountain by his righteous ones.

> I hear the Lord saying that in 2021 there is coming a shake-up and a shake-down to the cultural mountain of media.

"For My justice is a different justice, it is a righteous justice." says the Lord. "My ways are different than the worlds ways. My ways are perfect and my justice is true. See, not one person escapes my notice, not one heart is hidden from Me. My plans and purpose will prevail and My Truth will fill the air waves once again, releasing hope to the people. The enemy's schemes will come to naught as my sons and daughters rise up into the places I have called them within the media mountain."

The Holy Spirit showed me pictures of media outlets turning on one another as the Lord sends confusion into the enemy's camp. The Kingdom of God will begin to advance quickly into this mountain. As I watched this picture in my spirit, I saw one major door of opportunity opening; it was through this one door that chain-reaction breakthrough would begin.

I hear the Lord asking, "Who will stand in the gap? Who will intercede with persistent faith to see my Kingdom come in the media mountain?"

"I will raise up my righteous ones, my fire-branded ones to bring forth a new sound from the media mountain. In the coming days I will stir up a zeal for righteous standing and truth in this mountain. I will raise up sons and daughters who have willingly gone through My fires of transformation to reform this mountain. I see the wickedness and am raising up deliverers in this hour. As my sons and daughters begin to advance and move into position with their mouths full of my Spirit, they will birth a new sound, a sound that will become a holy trumpet, calling people to come up to the House of the Lord."

A Majestic God

There are not adequate words to describe the sheer magnitude, strength, power, and majesty of God. Who can fathom the depths of His love, the vastness of His faithfulness and mercy? The amazing thing is that, it is this God, who chooses to dwell in men, that transforms us into His image and likeness and uses us to see His Kingdom come on earth as it is in heaven.

In Jesus's name, I prophesy over you that the eyes of your heart will now be opened to see the one true living God—the Ancient of Days who never sleeps nor slumbers. The One whose breath of life is how we live and move and have our being. Holiness and radiant light emanate from His being and darkness cannot come near Him. May you see Him, the Lion of Judah, in all His splendor and encounter the fierce love that the true King of kings and Lord of lords has for you.

Rise up Kingdom warrior. Stand up and take the ground, cross the threshold, for you have been given the keys to overcome.

AUTHOR BIOGRAPHIES

Daneen Bottler and her husband Ty are dynamic apostolic and prophetic voices for this generation. Along with their two children Trenton and Kylie, they live in Portland Oregon, where they serve as Associate Senior Leaders of Father's House City Ministries. In addition to pastoring, the Bottlers are gifted musicians with a powerful anointing to release revelation of the majesty and fire of God through their music, drawing His body into profound expressions of worship and love for our great King. Their greatest desire is to see the glory of God displayed through His sons and daughters as they walk in their God-given power and authority. Ty and Daneen have had the privilege of speaking and ministering at various churches, conferences, and schools throughout the United States and Canada, releasing their apostolic and prophetic voices, encouraging unity within the body of Christ and seeing the Kingdom of God extended in authority and power. Their website is www.tyanddaneenbottler.com.

Curt Crook and his wife Susan both accepted Christ at a young age. Together they went to the mission field just after three years of marriage, when they were twenty years old. After returning to the States they became active in their home church, serving and ministering.

In 1980 Curt was ordained through Grace International. In 1984 he and Susan birthed Open Door Christian Fellowship under the oversight of Frank Damazio in Portland, Oregon. They pastored for twenty-six years before they turned leadership over to Curt's associate of eleven years. Curt has been a co-director of Revivalist School of Supernatural Ministries at Garden Valley Church in Roseburg, Oregon. He coached and trained there for four years, before stepping out as an entrepreneur and starting a successful Fresh Salsa Business. Susan is now a Supervisor at Douglas County, Oregon C.A.S.A. Curt continues to coach leaders, and their teams. He still leads teams into the nations and sees the supernatural work of God often in his dealings with people in the marketplace and in the course of life.

ANN FINLEY grew up with a Catholic background, in Lake Oswego, Oregon. Her genuine love and reverence for God became personal at the end of her sophomore year at University of Oregon, when she asked Jesus to be her Lord and Savior. Her intense hunger for more of God quickly led her to enroll at Portland Bible College in Portland, Oregon. Before the fall term, Ann attended a Bible Temple young adults retreat. It was there that she first witnessed the power of a prophetess in action. Ann didn't know anything about this spiritual office but knew in her heart that the Lord wanted her to run after and "jealousy desire" this gift! Directly following the retreat, Ann began her four years of Bible College. This is where she grew in her knowledge of the Word and the gifts of the Spirit. This too, is where Ann met her amazing husband, Don Finley. After graduating in 1984, they moved immediately to Salem, Oregon to work with Mike Herron at Willamette Christian Fellowship, a newly planted church. For several years they worked as youth pastors, worship pastors, and associate pastors, until in 1995 they became the senior leaders. In January, 2000, the church name changed to LIFE Church to more accurately reflect their message.

Ann has a vision to pursue the real life promised in Christ. Her prophetic voice and burden for freedom and transformation is communicated in her music, teaching, preaching, and praying. Some have described her passion as fiery and contagious. Ann is the leader over the prophetic department of LIFE Church. Through several years of training and trips to the "School of the Prophets" at Bethel Church and the Mission Church in Vacaville, CA, Ann's vision and desire has grown and been clarified. Her mission is to "Identify, Train, Empower, and Release the Prophetic through Relationship and Accountability." She has recently signed up to become a Certified Prophetic Trainer through Dan McCollam and Bethany Hick's "Prophetic Company" at the Mission Church. Ann's desire is for each of us to learn to hear our Lord's voice and be able to communicate it, not just as a "ministry skill" in church, but as a "life skill" where ever we go! This knowledge of who we are and to whom we belong will help us to change our environment as we assist in bringing heaven to earth through His supernatural power working in us.

BOBBY HAABY is a catalyst and thought leader who is encouraging and provoking the church to put "apostolic feet to prophetic hope." As a senior leader of Eagle Mountain, an Apostolic Resource Center in Bend, Oregon, Bobby thrives in creating an atmosphere where powerful people can run together and partner with God to release heaven on earth. Called to serve the Lord through an audible voice encounter, Bobby has given his life to see Christianity defined by the tangible presence of God, an atmosphere of training and discipleship, signs and wonders, and by releasing heavens blueprints for societal transformation that solves the worlds most pressing problems. Bobby operates from the belief that the world is desperate for an encounter with the living God and that we are witnessing the emerging of the sons and daughters that all creation has been waiting for. The kingdoms of this world are becoming the Kingdom of our God, and His Christ.

    Ministry: Eagle Mountain (Apostlic Resource Center)
    Website: eaglemountain.global

Podcast: Eagle Mountain Radio
YouTube: Eagle Mountain TV
EM Ministry FB Page: Eagle Mountain
Personal Ministry FB Page: Bobby and Becky Haaby
Personal FB Page: Bobby Haaby

DR. DAN C. HAMMER is a servant leader and visionary with a passion to reach the unloved with the gospel of Jesus Christ. Dr. Hammer is committed to intercessory prayer and uncovering the gifts of the Holy Spirit in the lives of believers. He regularly teaches how to attain life's full potential by understanding God's purpose for your life. Dr. Hammer is president of Seattle Bible College, and has taught there since 1984. He formerly served as Chancellor of Wagner Leadership Institute Seattle and is a member of the United States Coalition of Apostolic Leaders. He has traveled and ministered in thrity-seven nations.

Pastor Dan has a Bachelor of Theology from Seattle Bible College and a Master's and Doctorate from Bakke Graduate University. In 1986, He and his wife Terry planted Sonrise Christian Center (formerly Sonrise Chapel) as an independent Fellowship of Christian Assemblies in Everett, Washington, where they continue to serve as senior pastors. They have three adult children and six grandchildren.

HERB MARKS prayed the sinner's prayer on his knees at 4:00 AM Aug, 1971 in the middle of a dark street under a streetlight. Moments later he experienced hearing tens of thousands of angels worshiping God. This encounter marked his life to this day. A few years later he and two lovely women of God began a ministry for youth called "Sought Out." They focused on presentation of the Word with signs following. The ministry grew to include attendees from seventy-two churches representing eleven denominations. More than 5000 young people were influenced in this move of God. Today Sought Out meets in homes with people of all ages, and they are filled, sometimes with people overflowing into the back yard.

Herb is an associate pastor at Sonrise Christian Center located in Everett, Washington. He oversees the house of prayer where many miraculous answers to prayer have been recorded, from court cases being overturned to cancers disappearing. A baby boy in the womb was miraculously healed of a severe cleft palette and a hole in his heart. There are camera images of before and after the healing. Doctors said it couldn't happen, but through prayer it happened! Herb also oversees small group and home group gatherings, a major key for discipling people to face the unique challenges that are on the horizon for the church in this hour.

Sonrise Christian Center is looking forward into the future with great anticipation. It is a full gospel church bringing the Kingdom of heaven to earth. Herb and his wife Bethany have ministered together during their marriage of twenty-seven years. They love each other more now than the day they said "I do"! They have a twenty-one-year-old son named Deryck.

Herb is currently writing a book titled *Come Up Here*.

ABBEY MCCRACKEN is a young prophetic voice. She has been hearing God's voice since she was three years old, growing up in a prophetic household filled with testimonies of what God is doing. Her dad, Pastor Jeff McCracken (the coordinator of this book) has invited Abbey to travel and minister with him and she has been walking into her own ministry, anointing, and calling for years. In the Spring of 2020, Abbey graduated high school and college, simultaneously. She has recently been serving as an interim youth pastor and is going to Youth With A Mission (YWAM) in January 2021.

As Abbey has ministered in public schools, private schools,

ministry schools, churches, conferences, in the marketplace, and in social settings, her accuracy at such a young age has amazed leaders and recipients. She has a desire to walk in the fullness of her calling as a prophetic voice in the nations. From a very young age, she has desired to travel and minister around the world, excited to walk out biblical adventures of setting people free from their garbage and past. She is determined to speak life and encouragement into people, helping them to understand who God has designed them to be, not who they have been. She wants to see captives set free and walking in their godly, royal destinies. She wants them to walk in hope and a new perspective, not only of who they are but who God is.

JEFF MCCRACKEN is a husband, father, pastor, conference speaker, prophetic voice, and an apostolic leader. He is also an author with a growing body of work. Jeff's books include T*he Dangerous Book for Christians, Prophet Sharing 2020* and currently *Prophet Sharing 2021*. He has two new books that will be released in 2021: *Control* and *Jumpin' Ugly*. He believes that God is in a good mood and has good things to say to his kids, and Jeff desires to portray that to others with accurate and sometimes humorous prophetic insight. He couples word of knowledge with prophecy to reveal God's goodness. The Lord will usually give Jeff a word of knowledge (something that is current or past that Jeff couldn't know about the recipient without God's revelation) to reveal God's authenticity, presence, insight, and voice. Then God proceeds to share prophetic insight regarding the recipient's present and future. People are amazed by the accuracy and insight and often state that it is like Jeff has known them for years.

Jeff is a respected apostolic voice regionally, nationally, and internationally. He ministers in many nations throughout Europe and Asia, teaching schools on the prophetic, healing, strategic planning, and much more. He is also a respected voice on various boards and councils. He is a Council Member for the US Coalition of Apostolic Leaders (uscal.us) and a member of the International Coalition of Apostolic Leaders (icaleaders.com), the largest global gathering of apostolic leaders.

Pastor McCracken has had the honor of ministering globally to professional athletes, business leaders, military leaders, politicians, and church and denominational leaders. He has worked in ministry and business for more than thirty years and continues to consult for ministries, churches, and businesses. He is also a mentor, spiritual father, prophetic voice, and apostolic consultant to many leaders, churches and denominations in multiple nations.

Jeff and his wife RoxAnne are the senior leaders of Rainier Assembly of God in Rainier, OR. They are also the founders of the NW School of Supernatural Ministry, the Lower Columbia Healing Rooms, and the Hunger Network (a group of church, business and government leaders that are hungry for more of God and advancing the Kingdom of God). They have three adult children: Maddy, Ian, and Abbey.

KATHI PELTON and her husband Jeffrey understand our culture's need for encouragement and hope. Through writing and speaking, they escort individuals into awareness of God's profound compassion and mercy that heals brokenness, and they have a unique ability to help anyone seeking pathways into His kind embrace. For several years, Jeffrey and Kathi led "The War Room" in Kelowna, British Columbia, a house of prayer established by Patricia King and Donna Bromley. They continue to travel internationally, working with prayer and prophetic movements through their ministry Inscribe Ministries (website: inscribeministries.com). Kathi is also part of the leadership team for Watchmen for the Nations (watchmen.org) and is a well-respected prophetic voice who began writing for The Elijah List publication over a decade ago. She continues to write articles for The Elijah List and other prophetic newsletters, and contributes to various blogs and Christian publications. She is the author of the *30 Days to Breakthrough* book series, and has written two books with Jeffrey: *The Yielding: A Lifestyle of Surrender* and *The Sounds of Christmas.*

Jeffrey and Kathi were both born in northern California and lived there for many years, before the Lord moved them to the Portland, Oregon region. In 2019 the Holy Spirit began speaking to them about various ministry assignments they were to be involved in around and in Washingrton D.C. Early in January 2020, they relocated to Fredericksburg, Virginia, where they attend Awakening Community Church. They have four adult children and three grandchildren.

Dr. George Watkins is an apostle and prophet, and is director of Faith Producers Ministries. He has been holding crusades and leadership seminars and has helped establish churches in the nations of this world for over fifty years. George has taken teams to twenty-seven nations with him to duplicate himself into others. He loves to minister in radio broadcasting, audio and video ministry, as well as through a correspondence Bible course reaching into many countries of the world. He has authored several books: *Women in Today's Church*, a scriptural insight into God's intentions for both men and women to minister the Gospel of Jesus Christ; *Five Key Secrets to Long Life and Divine Health*, concerning God's supernatural protection and promises to those who obey Him; *Staying Free*, a mini-book used as a guide to maintaining freedom once delivered from the bondages of satan; *Ask The Boy*, stories through the eyes of those who were healed by the hands of Jesus; and *The Wisest Man I Have Ever Known*, stories and parables teaching the truths of God's word, as well as other teaching manuals.

Dr. Watkins received his doctorate degree from Beacon University in Columbus, Georgia. He loves to minister to the local church, has a heart for pastors, and is a seasoned veteran, pastoring his last church for twenty-nine years. George began his ministry as a teenage evangelist conducting church revivals and healing crusades, and this ministry has now spanned many decades. Multiple churches draw from his experience and consider him to be an integral part of their own ministries. His ministry is based on the belief that God means what He says, that His Word applies to our everyday, practical lives, and that it has power to make us whole in mind, body and soul. Dr. Watkins believes that the gifts of the Holy Spirit are to be used by every believer. He believes that using these spiritual tools will bring freedom to those in bondage, and his powerful prophetic ministry is a blessing to churches and the lives of individual people.

You can "walk" with George Watkins daily by visiting youtube.com/faithproducers; faithproducers.com; twitter.com/faithproducers; and facebook.com/faithporducerstv. His email is: faithproducers@gmail.com.

George and his wife Arlis live in Mount Vernon, WA and are the parents of three adult children: Tony, Tiffany, Corbin and their families.